MINNEAPOLIS
BURNING

MINNEAPOLIS BURNING

Did FBI agents protect the Minneapolis PD for years despite multiple warnings?

MICHAEL P. KEEFE

Copyright © 2022 Michael P. Keefe.

All rights reserved. No part of this book may be used or reproduced by any means, graphic, electronic, or mechanical, including photocopying, recording, taping or by any information storage retrieval system without the written permission of the author except in the case of brief quotations embodied in critical articles and reviews.

This is a work of creative nonfiction. While the vast majority of events are based on a true story, many of the names and characters are fictitious, events have been compressed and conversations have been reconstructed. The name of some real people and places do appear in the book, but the events and actions in this book are products solely of the author's imagination. The author expresses opinions and beliefs throughout the book.

Archway Publishing books may be ordered through booksellers or by contacting:

Archway Publishing
1663 Liberty Drive
Bloomington, IN 47403
www.archwaypublishing.com
844-669-3957

Because of the dynamic nature of the Internet, any web addresses or links contained in this book may have changed since publication and may no longer be valid. The views expressed in this work are solely those of the author and do not necessarily reflect the views of the publisher, and the publisher hereby disclaims any responsibility for them.

Any people depicted in stock imagery provided by Getty Images are models, and such images are being used for illustrative purposes only. Certain stock imagery © Getty Images.

ISBN: 978-1-6657-3356-4 (sc)
ISBN: 978-1-6657-3355-7 (hc)
ISBN: 978-1-6657-3357-1 (e)

Library of Congress Control Number: 2022921244

Print information available on the last page.

Archway Publishing rev. date: 12/07/2022

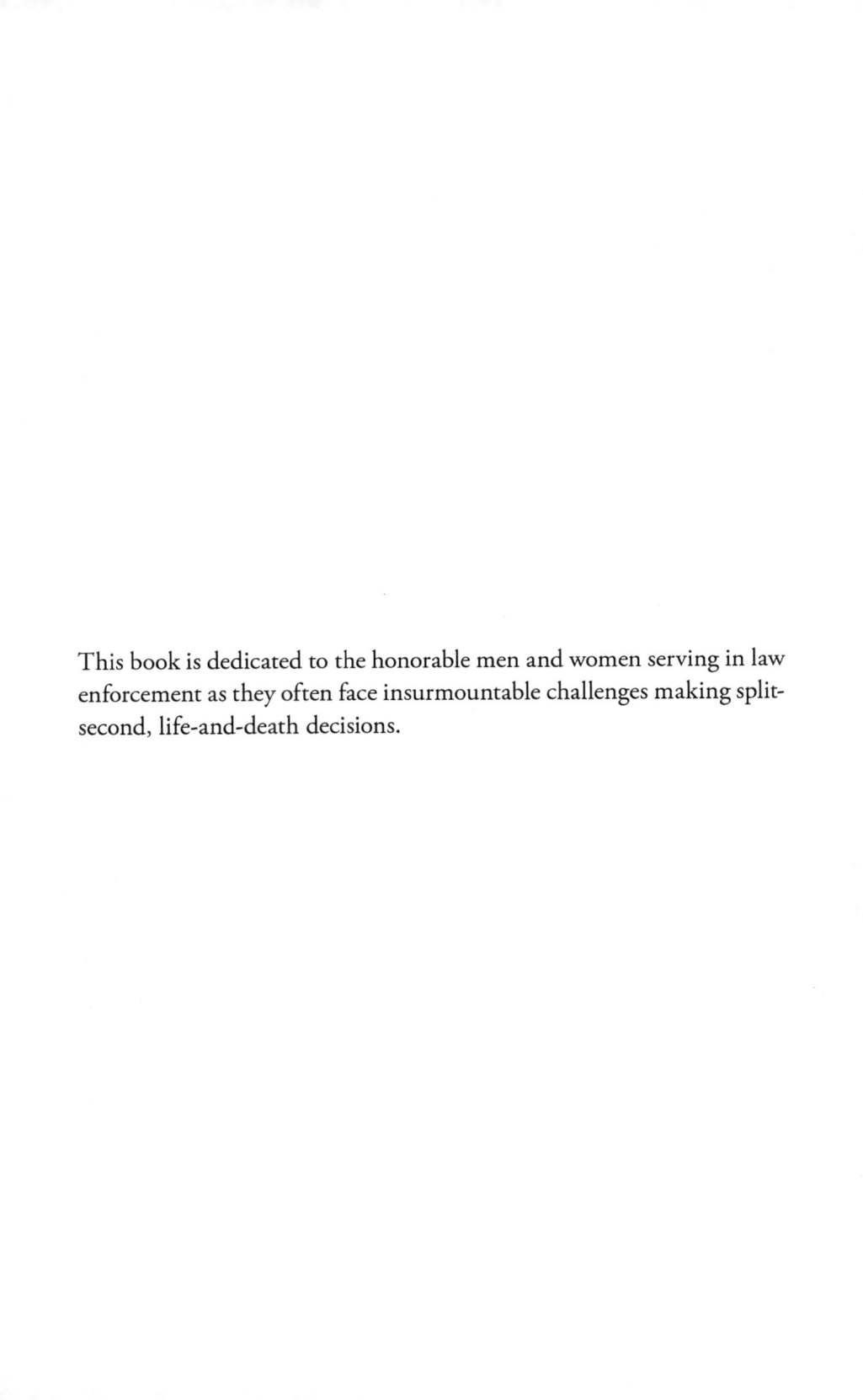

This book is dedicated to the honorable men and women serving in law enforcement as they often face insurmountable challenges making split-second, life-and-death decisions.

CONTENTS

Preface ix
Introduction xi

Chapter 1   The Informant 1
Chapter 2   The Raid 14
Chapter 3   Media Attack Number 1 23
Chapter 4   RICO Case 31
Chapter 5   FBI 40
Chapter 6   Media Attack Number 2 49
Chapter 7   Sergeant Burt 61
Chapter 8   City Hall Ambush 76
Chapter 9   The Missing Tape 85
Chapter 10 Internal Affairs Corruption 94
Chapter 11 Minneapolis Cop Cracks Under Pressure 103
Chapter 12 The Conspiracy 113
Chapter 13 Mississippi Burning 121
Chapter 14 The US District Court of Minnesota 129
Chapter 15 The Eighth Circuit Court of Appeals 138
Chapter 16 US Senate Judiciary 147
Chapter 17 Mayor Frey 159

Conclusion 167

PREFACE

This book is based on a true story about two veteran Minneapolis police officers who had the courage and integrity to "break the code," as a Minneapolis assistant city attorney jokingly put it one day at the First Precinct in downtown Minneapolis.

I, Lieutenant Michael Keefe, and Sergeant Paul Burt blew the whistle on corruption inside the Minneapolis Police Department, and a small number of other Minneapolis police officers and an FBI agent also spoke up and put their careers on the line because they, too, refused to turn a blind eye to the corruption in the MPD. Sgt. Burt and I have disciplined résumés based on years of service working in uniform as patrol officers and balanced out with years of service as detectives. That is the way it should be for everyone to move up the chain of command, but unfortunately that was not the case in Minneapolis. Many of the supervisors and commanders in the MPD worked the streets as uniformed patrol officers for a couple of years or less and then disappeared into the bureaucracy. They found cushy jobs as community resource cops or other plum assignments, all the while sucking up to the people in charge. Before long, they were promoted. They became clueless supervisors who had no idea what they were doing. It was a dangerous predicament and a formula for disaster, but unfortunately the pattern is all too common in the MPD and other police departments around the country, especially large ones.

Most were either too scared to work the streets as uniformed patrol officers or had never wanted to be real cops in the first place. Nevertheless, they couldn't wait to get into higher positions of power and authority.

The power and authority had attracted them to their jobs in the first place. Helping people was the last thing on their minds. Some quickly went from being cops to being politicians, and at that point, they became extremely dangerous. Every oath they ever took was tossed aside in favor of sucking up to whoever was in power and could help them climb the ladder. Some gave up on being cops and committed themselves to lying, cheating, and deceiving without hesitation. They willingly sat in front of clueless promotion boards, spilling a relentless salvo of self-aggrandizing lies without worrying about being caught or called on the carpet for their inflated egos and patently false, grandiose assessments.

Honest cops complained, but their complaints fell on deaf ears because those who made it to the top didn't give a damn about street cops who had been working as uniformed patrol officers for years. In due time, the mismanagement and corruption would eventually blow up, and the City of Minneapolis and the MPD would pay dearly for their misdeeds. The red flags were ignored, and I was persecuted.

The July 15, 2017, officer-involved shooting of Justine Damond and the May 25, 2020, in-custody death of George Floyd weren't just coincidence. Years of Minneapolis police commanders and politicians seemingly covering up evidence with the help of the Federal Bureau of Investigation turned the Minneapolis Police Department (MPD) into a ticking time bomb. It all might very well have been avoided if the powers that be had heeded my warnings and those who backed me up.

The senseless deaths of Justine Damond and George Floyd, as well as my own personal abuse at the hands of people in power in the City of Minneapolis, the MPD, the US attorney's office, and the FBI, inspired me, Lt. Keefe, to write this book.

INTRODUCTION

After graduating from high school, I enlisted in the US Air Force (USAF). I graduated from US Air Force basic military training at the top of my class and went on to receive a combination of medals and ribbons during my military career. My first USAF assignment was in Europe. I held a top-secret clearance due to my sensitive assignment and was stationed at USAF Headquarters, Ramstein Air Base, West Germany. I'm a lifetime member of the VFW and a member of my local American Legion. I attended the University of Minnesota, and I later graduated from the University of Nebraska at Omaha *cum laude*.

After leaving the USAF, I returned home and joined the MPD. Throughout my career, I was often in the middle of high-profile cases and assignments. In fact, the very first call of my career involved a man holding a knife to the throat of his girlfriend. Other officers and a sergeant arrived at the scene and shot and killed the man before I and my field-training officer arrived.

While in the police academy, recruits were asked to pick a precinct assignment. It wasn't any guarantee, but the department wanted officers working in areas of the city they preferred to work in. I picked the roughest and toughest assignment in Minneapolis, the Fourth Precinct. I saw it as a challenge, and I loved every minute of it.

My good friend from the academy, Steve McCarty, also picked the Fourth Precinct. We became partners and lifelong friends. We had two veteran sergeants, Tom McKenzie and Bruce McDonald. Most of McKenzie's superiors were intimidated by him. He was as tough as nails, and nobody pushed him. McDonald was also tough, but with a much more laid-back personality. The shift commander was a salt-of-the-earth man by the name of Bernie Bottema. Lt. Bottema was as good as they come, and everyone loved him.

During my time on the streets of North Minneapolis, I was made aware of some very corrupt and dangerous cops. Two were alleged to have been involved in a burglary ring and may have killed a fellow Minneapolis officer who was about to blow the whistle on them. The other one was a lieutenant who was allegedly raping prostitutes.

Several years later, a hardworking and honest Minneapolis cop whom I had known and worked with in the past confided in me and told me that he had literally caught one of the two cops involved in the burglary ring carrying a TV out of a house in South Minneapolis one morning. The officer told me he was slowly and quietly cruising alleys in his marked squad car at daybreak, looking for burglars and thieves, when he literally caught one of the officers in the act. He said they both stopped and locked eyes, and then the officer, who was in plain clothes, just walked off with the TV. A very senior officer told the officer to keep his mouth shut, and he did.

McCarty and I kept a close eye on the corrupt cops and simultaneously kept our distance. We came to work every day and served the citizens of Minneapolis with absolute dedication and discipline. In fact, McCarty worked so hard he never took so much as a sick day during his first twenty-one-plus years on the job. We worked in a district of the Fourth Precinct with another cop by the name of Larry Krebsbach. Krebsbach, like McCarty, was from St. Paul. Nothing bothered Krebsbach, no matter what happened.

One day while I was training a new recruit, Dean Milner, Homicide sent a teletype to every Minneapolis police squad car about a triple murder in South Minneapolis. The teletype listed several vehicles the suspect may be driving, so I cross-checked the license plates and registered owners and found one address in the Fourth Precinct. It was the killer's grandmother's house. I quickly directed Milner to the house, and when we arrived, Milner spotted the killer's SUV parked out front.

I immediately notified homicide that Milner and I had an eye on the vehicle, a red-and-white GMC Yukon, from an alley behind the grandmother's house. Within a few minutes, the SUV was on the move. I ordered Milner to get behind the SUV as I grabbed the mic and called for backup. I notified other officers that we were following the vehicle of the suspect in the triple murder in South Minneapolis, and the dispatcher immediately told all squads to hold all radio traffic. I relayed the vehicle description and location as we followed right behind. Being covert was no longer the plan. It was game time, and we wanted the killer to know we were coming after him. Within two minutes or less, we had a sea of flashing lights roaring up behind us as we drove down West Broadway. Once the backup squads pulled in behind us, I called out a felony car stop. The suspect pulled over and was taken out of the SUV at gunpoint. The timing of the arrest was crucial, because although the killer had just taken a shower after the murders, he left a spot of blood behind his ear that was vital evidence for the prosecution. The suspect had killed his girlfriend's mother, her young son, and the son's little friend. Three senseless and cowardly, horrific murders. Without the blood evidence, the killer may have walked away free.

I made hundreds of arrests during my career, but this was clearly the most rewarding. Every cop in the city had the same information as we did that day when that teletype came out, but Milner and I did all the cross-checking and proactively tracked down the killer. It was a proud moment for us, and Milner, like McCarty and Krebsbach, became a lifelong friend of mine.

As a street cop, I worked a lot of off-duty jobs in North Minneapolis. I knew everyone, and everyone knew me. One night while working off duty at a gas station, I recognized a guy wanted for murder. I told the clerk to lock the doors, and I took him down at gunpoint. On another occasion, I was working off duty at a homeless shelter and detox center near downtown Minneapolis when I heard chatter over the police radio about a rape, and as I listened, the suspect's description was given. A few minutes later, the suspect showed up at the shelter, and I arrested him at gunpoint.

After working the streets for several years, I was promoted to sergeant.

I worked in Investigations and then back on the street before eventually landing in the homicide unit. However, before I joined Homicide, I put together a landmark federal carjacking case with the help of assistant US attorney Cliff Wardlaw. The case was the first in the country in which the vehicle itself could be considered a weapon.

Prior to the case *United States v. Wright*, only the use of a gun or weapon per se would make stealing a vehicle a federal carjacking crime. But carjacking victims were being intentionally run over or dragged to death after getting caught in seat belts as they desperately tried to get out of their vehicles. The landmark case enabled federal prosecutors around the country to go after violent carjackers who were intentionally running over people or dragging them to death. Prosecutors were no longer limited to prosecuting only suspects with guns, knives, and other weapons for carjacking. They could now identify the vehicle itself as a weapon when the suspect intentionally tried to run over a victim or failed to stop when a victim was being dragged.

In Wright's case, a valet was parking cars at a restaurant in South Minneapolis when he suddenly saw a man jump into one of the cars he was parking. The valet tried to stop the suspect, but the suspect accelerated toward the valet and tried to run him over. The valet bounced off the hood of the stolen vehicle. State prosecutors declined to charge the case. They said it was just another auto theft, but I disagreed, and I took the case to the US attorney's office. Wardlaw agreed with me, and together we made history. Wardlaw prosecuted the case, and the suspect was found guilty and was sent to federal prison. Since then, prosecutors around the country have used it as case law for similar carjacking cases.

I enjoyed putting together cases and getting people to talk. While I was working as a property crimes detective, an old man walked into the Fifth Precinct one day and literally cried as he told me about the theft of his wife's flowerpot urn at a local cemetery. I was livid that anyone would do something so cruel and sick. My anger and motivation drove me to uncover a sophisticated case of flowerpot urns being stolen from cemeteries all over Minnesota, sold to secondhand dealers, and shipped to New York. The suspect had stolen more than a million dollars' worth of urns over several years. I eventually tracked down the suspect and sent him off to prison.

My hard work and dedication paid off in 2006 when my homicide partner, Sgt. Chris Thomsen, and I were named Minneapolis Police Investigators of the Year. In fact, during one homicide investigation, I treated a family member of a homicide victim with so much respect and compassion that the man came back into the homicide office and confessed to me that he himself had killed a woman and buried her body in northern Minnesota. Within an hour of the surreal confession, Thomsen and I and the suspect were on board a Minnesota State Patrol plane, heading deep into the forests of northern Minnesota.

The state patrol pilot landed the small plane on a snowy runway west of Duluth, and we were met by Minnesota Bureau of Criminal Apprehension agents, Aitkin County deputies, and their sergeant, Steven Sandberg. From there the caravan drove through the snowy countryside to the murder scene. The murder victim was under frozen, snow-covered branches. It was a somber moment as Minnesota BCA agents and Aitkin County deputies secured the scene and took custody of the suspect. Thomsen and I shook hands with the Minnesota BCA agents, deputies, and Sgt. Sandberg, and returned to Minneapolis.

A few years later, Sgt. Sandberg was killed in the line of duty.

In 2007, I was promoted to lieutenant and immediately assigned to the most prestigious job in the MPD, command of the MPD/FBI Violent Offender Task Force, a.k.a. VOTF. My superiors said one of the many reasons they wanted me in charge of the task force was because I wasn't afraid to speak my mind and they didn't want anybody pushing the MPD around.

After taking command of the task force, I quickly identified misconduct and refused to turn a blind eye. The suspected officers, agents, and attorneys denied everything and fought back. Within a matter of weeks, I was removed from my command, but I kept up the fight and built a criminal case against the suspects in a civil lawsuit I filed against them. I lost the civil case, but it allowed me to build a massive criminal case against several law enforcement officers An arbitrator eventually ruled that certain officers made false allegations about me, but the police department never held any of them accountable for their false statements. They were literally above the law.

As I fought them from a distance, I returned to investigations and eventually back to the street as a uniformed supervisor in the First Precinct. I preached the dangers of dealing with people who suffered from drug overdoses and entered a state of what became known as "excited delirium," and who later died after fighting with officers. I used my roll calls not just as information distribution sessions but for training as well. Drug overdoses were common in downtown Minneapolis, and I routinely preached how to properly deal with suspects experiencing drug overdoses after they fought with the police. I knew my enemies in the front office would love nothing more than for me to be the supervisor of a highly public in-custody death at the hands of the police, so I went to great lengths to teach my officers how to properly deal with drugged-up suspects who resisted arrest and fought with officers and how to save their lives after they were in custody.

It wasn't brain surgery, but there were crucial steps that officers needed to take to reduce the risk of suspects dying in police custody. At least two of those crucial steps were not taken on May 25, 2020.

On December 14, 2015, I chased down a man with a gun after a wild gang shoot-out in downtown Minneapolis after the bars closed. I saw one of the shooters running away from the scene of the shooting with a gun, and I chased him down a dark alley and ordered the man to drop his weapon. The man turned on me and slowly threw his loaded gun down. I was literally a split second away from shooting and killing the man when he turned on me, but my years of experience and training as a street cop and detective allowed me to give the young man one last breath to do the right thing.

It would have clearly been a justified shooting, but my enemies in the front office would have likely fed me to the cop-hating wolves in the media and withheld all the crucial evidence that justified the shooting.

Ironically, on the other hand, a highly respected sergeant by the name Ker Yang put me in for the police department's highest award, the Medal of Valor. Sgt. Yang was also a doctor. As a licensed psychologist, Yang just could not get over the incredible courage, strength, control, and bravery of a fifty-year-old cop chasing a young man with a gun down a dark alley after a shooting. But a few high-ranking police commanders were seemingly helping cover the tracks of the cops I turned in for misconduct, so I was initially denied the medal.

CHAPTER 1
THE INFORMANT

IN MARCH 2007, AFTER SPENDING THE PAST FIVE YEARS AS A HOMICIDE detective, I was promoted from sergeant to lieutenant and assigned to take over as the commander of the Minneapolis Police Department's Violent Offender Task Force, commonly known as VOTF. The task force was made up of Minneapolis police officers; agents from the Bureau of Alcohol, Tobacco, Firearms and Explosives (ATF); and FBI agents. Hennepin County deputies also assisted at times.

The first major case I oversaw was a wiretap investigation of the Tre-Tre Crips street gang. The gang was operating in Minneapolis and Faribault, Minnesota. After a lengthy investigation, the gang was eventually crippled, and the gang's leaders were sent to prison. The ATF agent in charge of Minnesota, Bernard Zapor, gave me and my officers and agents awards for the successful operation. Zapor and former Minnesota US attorney Rachel Paulose personally came to the VOTF office and presented the medals, along with Hennepin County sheriff Rich Stanek and Minneapolis police chief Timothy Dolan. However, the operation, code-named Rolling Rock, was not without controversy. Officer safety became a contentious issue after two highly respected VOTF officers told me that the Tre-Tre Crips had threatened to kill a cop the next time they were stopped in Faribault. Furthermore, the officers, John Biederman and Timothy Eck, also told me they had personally watched one-person squads in Faribault make traffic stops on the Tre-Tre Crips.

As a patrol officer, I had spent several years working the streets of North Minneapolis during a time when Minneapolis was dubbed "Murderapolis," and I was very familiar with the unpredictable and violent nature of the Tre-Tre Crips and many other Minneapolis street gangs. Additionally, I had just spent the past five years working as a homicide detective, and several of my homicide cases involved gangs. I took this threat seriously. I knew the Crips were unpredictable and extremely dangerous. In fact, one night while we had them under surveillance in St. Paul, they opened fire on a rival gang. In another incident, they shot a rival gang member in Faribault. I notified ATF supervisor Samuel Lawson and assistant US attorney Anders Folk about my concerns for the safety of Faribault police officers, Rice County deputies, and Minnesota state troopers, so we met in the ATF office in St. Paul.

During that meeting, I argued we should notify Faribault chief of police Mike Lewis and Rice County sheriff Richard Cook. Lawson immediately objected. I refused to back down and told Folk, "If one of those cops gets killed, it will be on you, Anders." Anders Folk never hesitated. Folk was a former US Marine officer and he understood. He immediately told me to brief the Faribault chief and the Rice County sheriff. Folk said he would minimize the chief and sheriff within a couple of days and provide them with the details of the federal wiretap.[1]

Lawson was convinced that if the authorities in Faribault were briefed, the case would be compromised. I considered this ridiculous and irrational, and I made it clear to Lawson I did not agree with his theory. This was now the second time that Lawson and I had butted heads. The first time was earlier, during the wiretap, when Lawson asked me to place my officers and agents on twenty-four-hour coverage in the event they overheard the Tre-Tre Crips take part in a shooting or something similar. I told Lawson that if the officers in the wire room overheard something like that and it required a 911 response, the proper thing to do would be to immediately notify the local police in the applicable jurisdiction so

---

[1] "Minimize" is a legal term meaning "To engage in the process of providing confidential information to select law enforcement officers, agents, and attorneys about a sensitive case."

that they could quickly and safely respond with appropriate backup. I also reminded Lawson that the Crips were dealing drugs and guns over a large area that covered more than three counties, and odds were we would never be able to respond in a timely manner anyway. Moreover, in any emergency situation, local officers would likely be responding to shots fired or a shooting, and to interject undercover officers into that scenario would only make things worse and unnecessarily endanger the lives of the undercover officers and the responding officers as well.

I suspected that unethical and overtime-hungry VOTF officers went behind my back and prodded Lawson to ask me to do this because it would have offered them a great deal of overtime. Federal agents do not get overtime. Their overtime is expected and part of their salary. Regardless, I thought it was a foolish idea. Besides, my officers and FBI agents were secretly working on a public corruption case that Lawson had no knowledge of. Furthermore, I did not have the available personnel to carry out what I thought was a reckless plan. As a uniformed street cop, I had experienced several cases of undercover narcotics officers abruptly calling for backup after a drug deal went bad. It was always absolute pandemonium and extremely dangerous. Undercover officers running around with guns drawn is always a precarious situation, and unfortunately officers have been killed by friendly fire when they have shown up on calls with guns drawn because uniformed officers don't know who friend or foe is.

It seemed to me that Lawson did not understand that interjecting undercover officers with guns drawn into the middle of a dangerous 911 call, such as one involving shots fired or a shooting with responding uniformed officers, was inherently dangerous and potentially deadly. Lawson and his supervisor, Gary Pedowski, were beside themselves. They'd had two disagreements with me, and they'd lost both. Their insecurity led Pedowski to send me an email telling me I was banned from the St. Paul ATF office. I laughed it off, but I later found out that this is a game federal agencies play when they don't get their way. Anyway, Pedowski eventually calmed down and sent me an apology. He offered to buy me a beer and said he considered the matter over and done with, but I would later find out that was not the case.

Informing local officers would have been ideal

Posted: Friday, June 22, 2007 12:00 am

The Bureau of Alcohol, Tobacco, Firearms and Explosives played a dangerous game with our local police department in the level of secrecy it kept with Operation Rolling Rock, an effort that it believes took some seriously bad guys off the street.

Some details: The ATF started this drug and weapons investigation about eight months before a May 20 shooting in Faribault that sparked an increasing troublesome series of events. According to Faribault Police Chief Mike Lewis, the feds told the locals about the operation just three weeks before the shooting, more than seven months after the investigation began.

So what you had were undercover federal agents mingling in dangerous environments with undercover local police officers without anyone knowing who the others truly were. When you start thinking about how brazen these violent bad guys got in the days leading up to the final sweep of Operation Rolling Rock, you realize that it is extremely fortunate none of the good guys got hurt - at the hands of other good guys.

Think of this scenario: The federal undercover agents are in the drug den that both federal and local agencies knew about. Something goes wrong with a buy and guns are drawn. The local police receive a call about this and respond to the incident. They draw their weapons. Now who are the bad guys? Without any knowledge that there were federal good guys around, the situation would have been a powder keg.

We come back to a common theme we have in this space: Communication. We understand all about the integrity of the federal investigation and how the ATF might have been hesitant to provide their information more than they felt absolutely necessary. But when you start putting law enforcement agents - local or federal - in danger because of this secrecy you step into dangerous territory.

We're appreciative of what Operation Rolling Rock did for our community, taking what appears to be some seriously bad guys off the street. We just feel fortunate we're not reporting on a friendly-fire incident that occurred in the process.

Faribault DAILY NEWS, JUNE 22, 2007

Another case I oversaw in 2007 was a public corruption case involving a convicted drug dealer by the name of B. B. Jackson. Jackson caught the attention of the MPD and the FBI after a longtime MPD homicide informant came forward and claimed Jackson was bragging he had corrupt MPD cops on his payroll. He was allegedly giving the corrupt officers money or prostitutes in exchange for classified police information. The MPD and the FBI acted on the information because the informant had a reputation of providing reliable intelligence. So VOTF officers and agents sold Jackson cocaine, and after several deals Jackson was arrested at the end of June 2007. The goal was to find out whether Jackson was lying or whether he really did have cops on the take.

The arrest of Jackson went bad after the FBI refused to let uniformed Hennepin County deputies arrest him when he was watering his lawn. It was the perfect opportunity to take him down, but it was not part of the FBI's operations plan. VOTF officers and agents watched Jackson walk around his yard, but the FBI was calling the shots on this arrest. The FBI stopped the officers, agents, and deputies from moving in and making the arrest. It seemed ridiculous, and undercover Minneapolis officers and deputies complained to me about the FBI and its antiquated system of micromanaging its agents.

Finally, Jackson left his house and VOTF officers and agents followed him as he headed toward Minneapolis. I was the field commander as undercover cars circled all around Jackson. Jackson appeared carefree as he cruised down Minnesota Highway 55, totally oblivious to all the undercover agents and officers preparing to converge on him.

The only problem was that one of the uniformed Hennepin County deputies had to go to his kid's baseball game, so another deputy took him to the ballpark. Murphy's law was in full force, but the lone deputy quickly caught up to the undercover officers as they reached the western edge of Minneapolis. The delay allowed Jackson to get inside the city of Minneapolis, which is what everyone was trying to avoid. So as soon as the marked squad was in position and it was safe to do so, I gave the order to take Jackson down. Jackson was already deep into North Minneapolis, and other drug dealers and users saw undercover officers and the uniformed deputy in a marked squad take him into custody. It was the last thing the FBI and I wanted, but there was nothing we could do. Jackson was taken into custody and transported to the Minneapolis FBI office.

From there Jackson launched a salvo of lies and fairy tales after assistant US attorney Henry Stahl asked him whether he had anything to offer—like cops. It was a stupid move, which Stahl was advised not to do, but he did it anyway. Jackson was backed into a corner. The lightbulb went off, and away he went; he wasn't about to go back to federal prison as long as he had a gullible assistant US attorney in front of him. Jackson threw out lie after lie about cops he knew from high school and his old neighborhood, and cops who worked off duty at a bar he frequented. I was able to refute virtually everything Jackson said, but the FBI and Stahl seemingly didn't care. They wanted a career-building case, and this was the perfect opportunity.

Within three weeks of Jackson's arrest, Detective Logan Preston told VOTF sergeants Karl Eklund and John Haverly that Jackson had changed his original story regarding the identity of one of the officers Jackson had originally claimed was corrupt on the night of his arrest. The sergeants immediately told me, and I wasn't surprised, because in my view Jackson had been lying and playing games from the moment he was taken into custody. Sgt. Haverly agreed with me and asked me to be present for the next interview. A few days later, Officer Preston notified me that he planned to reinterview Jackson on July 25, 2007, at an FBI safe house, and he requested our presence. Preston knew this was serious business, and he wanted higher-ranking officers calling the shots.

Everyone met at the FBI safe house. FBI agent Jay Luden was already interviewing Jackson when Haverly and I arrived, and we could plainly see that Jackson was spinning Luden around like a top. It was fingernails on the blackboard for me and Haverly to watch a career criminal spin his tangled web of deceit. Haverly and I had seen this game many times before as veteran street cops and detectives.

When Luden was done letting Jackson make a fool out of him, Haverly asked me to step in and interview Jackson. I immediately put

Jackson at ease by bringing up Jackson's old neighborhood and people we both knew from North Minneapolis. I allowed Jackson to brag about himself and pretended I was impressed and equally enamored. Jackson took the bait just as Luden had taken Jackson's bait, but this time it was a veteran detective flipping the script on an arrogant career criminal who thought every cop and federal agent was gullible. Haverly and I, unlike Luden, had seen more than our fair share of desperate "informants" backed into corners.

Once we had Jackson at ease, I segued into the public corruption case, and Jackson proceeded to tell me, Haverly, Preston, Luden, Agent Jim Tracy, and an FBI analyst one outlandish story after another regarding the so-called corrupt officers. Within a matter of minutes, I had Jackson contradicting himself on significant details he had claimed were 100 percent spot-on when he was arrested. Jackson was changing the names of officers he had said were corrupt on the night of his arrest. If it hadn't been a joint MPD/FBI case, I would have immediately arrested Jackson on the spot and booked him into the Hennepin County Jail for obstructing justice and several other potential crimes. Jackson's bogus claims were obvious and blatant, and I had no time for that. This was serious business. Assistant US attorneys made it very clear that if Jackson lied, the deal was off and he would no longer be used as a "cooperating defendant" and would be sent back to prison. It was very clear to me that Jackson was lying, and in my opinion, Jackson's reckless and uncorroborated stories warranted an immediate suspension of the case.

There was nothing more to talk about. I would later tell Captain Francis Miller that only an absolute idiot would believe such obvious lies. Not only that, but Jackson's new version of "corrupt officers" was a complete flip-flop from his original story. It was an absolute no-brainer; Jackson was not being truthful. He claimed six officers were corrupt: four black, one Hispanic, and one white.

Jackson was so full of himself. He was trying to convince us he was connected to Mexican drug cartels and the highest-ranking gang members in Chicago. Jackson claimed he could move several kilos of cocaine from California to Minnesota and everything else he could dream up, but apparently he forgot he had been caught buying small amounts of cocaine from undercover Minneapolis cops and FBI agents just a few weeks before. If he was such a big-time drug kingpin why was he buying small amounts of cocaine in Minneapolis? It was just another ridiculous lie, and despite its foolishness, the FBI, MPD, and US attorneys backed him up.

I later told this to the DEA, and they just laughed. It was nothing but self-aggrandizing bull—— by a desperate man doing everything possible to avoid being sent back to federal prison. I also told Capt. Miller that in my opinion Jackson had violated his court-mandated agreement to tell the truth, and I felt as though the FBI was trying to gloss over Jackson's crazy stories and ridiculous allegations. Jackson's wild and contradictory stories were exculpatory evidence that I felt the FBI was required to tell the court.

I made it clear to Capt. Miller and the FBI that I felt Jackson had violated the conditions of his court order to be an honest cooperating defendant. In my mind, Jackson was nothing but a con man looking to save himself from another trip to federal prison, and I wasn't fooled for one minute, and neither was Haverly or Miller. Jackson's court-ordered agreement, as it was explained to me and others, should have been nullified as soon as Jackson changed his stories regarding the officers he claimed were corrupt. I briefed the FBI supervisor, Bryce Turner, after our interview of Jackson at the FBI safe house. The FBI briefing took place at about two o'clock on the same day at the Minneapolis FBI office. Per the law and FBI policy, the case was legally over when Jackson lied—end of story.

Jackson's accusations were not a simple misunderstanding, and I documented everything in detail. There was no room for error in my summary of the interview, and if anyone from the MPD or FBI said anything to the contrary, he was not being honest. I was standing on a big rock, and the FBI knew it. I wasn't backing down. Jackson was not conforming to the truth, and I was the commander of VOTF. I had an impeccable career as a detective, and I wasn't about to bend the rules for anyone or any agency.

I lowered the boom on the FBI a few days later in a VOTF staff meeting when I notified my officers and FBI agents that the Minneapolis Police Department (MPD) was not about to skirt the rules of criminal procedure. If the FBI wanted to continue with the case against the officers they would have to do it on their own. The MPD was out. Sgt. Haverly and I were not about to compromise ourselves, our badges, or the City of Minneapolis. It was over, and I drew a line in the sand.

Unfortunately, this was the start of arguably one of the biggest and most sophisticated cases of public corruption in American history. Law enforcement officers, agents, and attorneys who were supposed to be investigating corruption quickly flipped the script and, within a matter of minutes, seemingly made themselves suspects in a racially motivated attack on black police officers. The Hispanic officer who looked white and the white officer were placed on the back burner.

Sgt. Haverly and I demanded transparency and accountability, but subordinate cops and agents did not want the case shut down, because they were seemingly motivated by racial antipathy or the promise of unlimited overtime and career advancement. The unlimited and unaccountable overtime was a huge motivating factor for lower-ranking officers because that money was added to their pensions. Many of them are today, or will be, receiving a six-figure pension. Haverly and I didn't give a damn about the money, but the loss of overtime money was a serious threat to the current and future income of some officers, so they had to come up with a plan to get me removed from their command.

The first thing they had to do was recruit and dupe high-ranking FBI agents into believing I would tip off, or already had tipped off, black cops about the public corruption case. The second thing they needed to do was sell the same bogus story to the MPD command staff, because the FBI had no authority to remove me without the authorization of the Minneapolis police command staff. In my mind, it was an easy sell to the incompetent and unethical commanders on both sides. They didn't need the money. They were already making well over six figures, with take home-cars to boot.

The task force bylaws were very clear—I was in charge of the cops and federal agents. Furthermore, the entire unit was housed in a secure City of Minneapolis building. I demanded the "public corruption" case be shut down because, in my opinion, Jackson was clearly misleading everyone about a massive case of corruption involving MPD cops.

I felt as though Jackson was simply trying to avoid a second tour of duty with the Federal Bureau of Prisons. The FBI knew I was right, but they apparently didn't care. They wanted the case to continue, so they sent two high-ranking agents to go behind my back and tell Deputy Chief Edward Parker that I had interviewed Jackson without their "approval" and that they wanted me removed from the task force. They claimed I was interfering in the case. It was all nonsense. I was the commander, and I had every right to interview Jackson; and when I did so, I caught Jackson in several lies and demanded that the public corruption case end on July 31, 2007.

Deputy Chief Parker agreed with the FBI. Without ever talking to me, Parker removed me from my command. I believe this could have been the FBI's first act of criminal misconduct. The FBI went behind my back and falsely claimed I was interfering in a public corruption case. I, as the commander of VOTF, had every right to make sure the rules of criminal procedure were being followed. It was my job. Furthermore, my officers came to me and complained that Jackson was "lying."

If I had miscarried in any way, why didn't the FBI confront me? I never miscarried or failed in my duties as the VOTF commander, so they stabbed me in the back and falsely claimed I had. On the other hand, the FBI miscarried and did an end-around because they knew I would not help them cover up Jackson's lies. And the greedy cops under me saw it as an opportunity to cash in big time with unlimited overtime.

It's likely that the Minneapolis VOTF cops encouraged the FBI to go to Deputy Chief Parker in the first place, but regardless, the FBI rolled dirty. They stepped in it big time, and there was no turning back. As time went on, they dug a deeper hole. The FBI was required by policy to contact the senior prosecutor and advise him or her of an informant's misconduct, and the Minneapolis FBI office was required to notify FBI headquarters. Apparently none of this happened, or if it did, the ring of corruption just got bigger. Robert Mueller was the director of the FBI in 2007, and Roberto R. Gonzales was the US attorney general. Did Mueller of Gonzales or one of their deputies give the Minneapolis FBI field office the green light to cover up Jackson's seemingly false statements and stab me in the back with the help of the MPD? Or did the buck stop with the acting US attorney for Minnesota, or the Minneapolis FBI special agent in charge? It's a question that needs to be answered, because it's the backbone of the seeming corruption.

In my mind, the FBI and Deputy Chief Parker partnered up with VOTF officers to go after black cops without an ounce of legitimate probable cause. I felt that Parker threw me under the bus and gave the FBI what they wanted. Regardless, they had to come up with a reason to remove me, because I was doing the right thing and following the rule of law and the conditions of Jackson's court-mandated agreement. The first plan was to offer me a promotion to captain and another assignment, but I immediately turned it down. So they came up with plan B, which was a cover story that claimed I had miscarried in the previous MPD/ATF case in Faribault, for which I and my officers and agents had been given awards. What was going on? None of it made any sense.

Who was behind this nonsense and blatant stupidity? It didn't matter. I felt that the FBI and Deputy Chief Parker stabbed me in the back for doing my job and following the letter of the law. This act on the part of FBI agents, Parker, and several other officers and agents was arguably the birth of one of the biggest cases of police corruption in the history of American law enforcement, according to retired FBI agent Dan Vogel and several other career law enforcement officers. Never before in American history, they believed, have cops, FBI agents, and assistant US attorneys been caught covering up exculpatory evidence—Jackson's lies—to manufacture a case and persecute the whistleblower who tried to stop it.

After I was removed from my command, I demanded an interview with Deputy Chief Parker and Major Wesley Yates. I demanded to know why I had been removed. Parker initially relayed the bogus cover story, and I refuted everything he said. Finally, out of frustration, Parker pointed his finger at me and said, "Don't tell them I told you, but they [the FBI] were really mad about that interview with Jackson." Translation: Parker wasn't supposed to tell me the real reason for my removal from the task force. The silly cover story was supposed to be confidential, but I flipped Parker into a confession. It was all bunk!

My first thought was *So what? Why didn't you back me up?* I couldn't believe a career police officer didn't seem to have the courage or integrity to tell the FBI he would gather the facts and get back to them. On the contrary, I felt he threw me under the bus just as he had thrown the FBI under the bus a few seconds prior, when I refuted all his lies surrounding the ridiculous cover story. Parker was weak and incompetent. He was on the wrong team and he knew it, but he dug his heels in anyway and refused to give me back my command of VOTF.

Deputy Chief Parker was in bed with the FBI. He had to have known that what they did was wrong. But it was too late. The two high-ranking FBI agents who came to Parker and Yates created a massive case of criminal conspiracy, but it quickly fell apart when Parker told me not to say anything. It was all haphazard and just plain dumb, but the longer it went on, the more dangerous it became. The hole they dug just kept getting bigger. They thought I would back down, but I never did.

I believe some of the motivation behind getting rid of me was nothing other than money and power. The cops wanted the unlimited overtime the public corruption case offered. The FBI agents and assistant US attorneys saw it as a great opportunity for career advancement. They would be promoted based on successful major cases, and taking down cops was the crème de la crème of major cases. They apparently were not about to follow the proper rules of criminal procedure to get the job done. I was in their way, and I had to go.

I had caught Jackson in multiple lies that violated every aspect of the court-mandated agreement. The case was supposed to be immediately shut down—end of story. It was FBI policy and the law. Everyone was told by assistant US attorneys Stahl and Schultz that Jackson would be immediately sent back to prison if he lied, and lie he did. Specifically, Jackson changed the names of the six officers he initially claimed were corrupt. When he did, Sergeant Matthew Bright was now allegedly one of the corrupt officers. Bright and two high-ranking commanders were fierce enemies.

There was no way they were going to put up with any of the VOTF sergeants or my investigative demands now. It was time to remove me and let the FBI go after whomever they wanted. The only problem was that they knew I was right in demanding accountability, transparency, and strict adhesion to the rules of criminal procedure.

They had to get rid of me so that they could let the FBI carry on with their illegitimate case, so in their tangled web of lies and deceit, they spontaneously hatched the infamous cover story. The cover story was poorly designed, and it all fell apart on August 20 when I confronted Deputy Chief Parker and Major Wesley Yates. But apparently Officer Jack Hardy and others never got word that Parker seemed to confess to me, because according to Internal Affairs sergeant Gemma Shaw, Hardy walked into Internal Affairs a few weeks later and swore it was all true. The infamous cover story laid the framework for a massive Title 18 criminal case of conspiracy to obstruct justice, and several other crimes that I would allege.

CHAPTER 2
THE RAID

Prior to the meeting on August 20, I sent Parker a detailed four-page letter regarding VOTF overtime abuse and the bizarre behavior of the ATF supervisors Lawson and Pedowski. I also noted that supervisory FBI agent Steve Walters had warned me not to trust ATF agent Lawson and to keep all confidential FBI documents out of his hands. After I sent Parker the letter, we agreed to meet in his office on August 20 regarding my transfer out of VOTF.

During that meeting, during which Major Wesley Yates was also present, Parker initially tried to sell me what I felt was a cover story and the transfer of a subordinate as the reason for my transfer, but I refuted everything Parker said. I made Parker look like a fool, and I believe he knew it. He was trying to convince me, the man he helped make investigator of the year in 2006, that he was doing what he had to do because I allegedly miscarried in the MPD/ATF case. I looked at Parker and Yates with contempt and disgust, and I knew it upset them. I refused to show either one of them any respect. They didn't deserve it.

I would later learn the names of the two high-ranking FBI agents who met with Parker and asked him to remove me after I caught Jackson changing his stories on July 25. That move on the part of the FBI is universally viewed by criminal defense attorneys as a very serious criminal act. FBI agents going behind the back of a high-ranking police commander to stop him from exposing exculpatory evidence so that they can seemingly cover it up and direct the course of a case could be found to be serious criminal misconduct, and perhaps a Racketeer Influenced and Corrupt Organizations (RICO) case. RICO cases are generally used to combat organized crime in the United States, but they can also be used to indict and arrest law enforcement officers that have conspired to obstruct justice under the color of law.

Years later Officer Joe Denton told me and my attorneys during his deposition that he thought the two high-ranking FBI agents were Bryce Turner and R. J. Alinsky. This would make sense, because I recalled their presence on the night Jackson was taken into custody.

Several years ago, a national news organization exposed an FBI agent by the name of R. J. Alinsky for allegedly making false statements in a criminal case. The judge in the case said Alinsky provided false testimony and was a fourteen-year veteran of the FBI in 2004. Was this the same agent who went to Parker with agent Turner and told him I should be removed from my command? Was Alinsky removed from his previous FBI field office and sent to Minneapolis? This might explain why the FBI has refused to police itself. Did they have a high-ranking agent in Minneapolis who should have been terminated years earlier? These are reasonable questions that need to be answered.

At any rate, before I left the meeting I tore into Parker and Yates, but neither one cared. I believe they knew that what they were doing was criminal, but they didn't care because they were on the FBI's team. They were in power, and nobody was going to touch them. Keep in mind that Yates was sitting right next to Parker when he admitted to me that the cover story was a hoax. The infamous cover story becomes very important as time goes on and the lies continue.

The FBI safe house interview should have ended the so-called public corruption case, and Jackson should have been sent back to prison, but high-ranking FBI agents and Minneapolis police commanders kept it alive. On the night of his arrest, Jackson identified six Minneapolis police officers as being corrupt, and he was adamant about their identities. I insisted the FBI show Jackson their photographs and make him confirm their identities because I knew Jackson was not being honest and nothing he was saying made sense. But FBI agent Jay Luden told me they didn't have any photographs available in the FBI office. Needless to say, only a fool would believe such nonsense. The postarrest interview of Jackson should have been audio and video recorded, and Jackson should have been made to sign confirmatory photos of the officers he claimed were corrupt. This was standard practice in Minneapolis and around the country for even the simplest, most mundane crimes in 2007 and before, yet the FBI did none of the above because they apparently wanted to control the direction of their case. They wanted to make it fit.

Years later, my lawyers and I would confirm Jackson grew up in the same neighborhood as two of the officers he claimed were on the take, so how could he misidentify two guys he grew up with? They were two brothers, in fact, one much taller than the other, and one of them beat Jackson up when they were kids. Yet Jackson was having amnesia as to who was who. Everyone Jackson identified was someone he either grew up with or went to school with, or someone he knew from a bar where they worked as off-duty police officers.

Jackson's stories only got worse as the FBI continued with its perilous case. On August 9, 2007, the FBI placed Jackson in front of Officer Mike Roberts while Roberts was working off duty in downtown Minneapolis. On the night of his arrest, Jackson initially said Roberts routinely ran license-plate checks for him in exchange for money, and that seemed plausible. However, when it came time for Jackson to approach Officer Roberts and ask him to run a license plate for money, he didn't know who Officer Roberts was as he stood on the street in full MPD uniform.

This was now at least the third time Jackson misidentified officers he claimed were corrupt. During the FBI safe house interview, Jackson switched the names of two of the initial six officers he claimed were corrupt, and he added two more, and he couldn't even identify Officers Roberts. In no uncertain terms, if this is true, and I believe it is, the FBI should have immediately placed Jackson under arrest and ended everything right there and then, but they didn't.

On the night of Jackson's arrest, he said Officer Roberts was the tall cop at North High School, but that was actually another officer. Nevertheless, Jackson insisted that the name of the corrupt school cop was

Officer Roberts, so the FBI placed him on the street in front of Officer Roberts, but Jackson did not recognize Roberts. Jackson literally did not recognize or know Officer Roberts, so they allegedly had to get a third party, Frankie Harris, to introduce the two men to one another. After the introduction, Officer Roberts ran a license plate for Jackson and accepted money from Jackson, so Roberts was arrested, charged, convicted, and sent to prison for accepting a bribe. With that bit of luck came the end of the precarious FBI case, but they still had the problem of dealing with all the potential crimes they had committed along the way and the fear that I would tell the world how they seemingly covered up exculpatory evidence to keep the case alive. The apparent criminal misconduct on the part of the FBI, the MPD, and assistant US attorneys would only get worse as panic set in, but not before VOTF officers and agents endangered the lives of MPD officers and nearly killed an innocent family.

R. T. Rybak was the mayor of Minneapolis from 2002 until 2014. He was always pleasant whenever he saw me and other officers in uniform coming and going from city hall. Rybak most likely didn't know me by name when I was in uniform, but he obviously recognized me years later when I and another plainclothes detective, Sergeant Stuart Helmer, were walking through the Pillsbury Building, which was kitty-corner from city hall. If looks could kill, I would be a dead man. Rybak's generally friendly demeanor was gone. By now Rybak was surely aware of who I was after seeing my picture in the newspaper and on TV.

I suspect that Rybak and his chief of staff, Tina Smith, were most likely misled by high-ranking police commanders and the city attorney's office. Regardless, when a high-ranking police commander blows the whistle and says there is corruption inside a major metropolitan police department, common sense would dictate that the mayor would ask some questions. And maybe he did. But nobody from the mayor's office ever sat down with me to hear what I had to say. Smith went on to become Minnesota's lieutenant governor and eventually was elected to the US Senate. Today Smith is one of Minnesota's two US senators.

At any rate, in 2007 the City of Minneapolis was $6 million in the red, and city leaders turned to the police department to make up the shortfall.

This caused some VOTF officers a great deal of stress. To make matters worse, some officers were no longer entitled to receive any more federal overtime pay, because they had already maxed out their 2007 federal overtime benefit of $15,600 by the middle of the summer. The only overtime pay they could get now was from the city, and the city was saying they could have no more overtime pay. The only exception was the public corruption case. If the public corruption case ended, so did all their overtime, and some of them were not about to let that happen without a fight.

The greedy VOTF officers desperately wanted me and my sergeants out the door so they could keep pulling in their unlimited and unaccountable overtime and keep their government cars, but I never miscarried, so they had to come up with an excuse to get rid of me first because I was the decision-maker. I was the one putting the brakes on the case and their overtime. They literally panicked when I told them I was not going to cover up any exculpatory evidence. I made it clear we were no longer going to support the FBI after I caught Jackson repeatedly misstating facts and telling wild, self-aggrandizing stories. I had expected the FBI to support me and follow the rules of criminal procedure, but they went in another direction.

I believe a few of the VOTF officers saw this as a great opportunity to stab me in the back and get in bed with the FBI. The end of the public corruption case meant no more overtime and no more take-home cars for some VOTF officers. The majority of officers on task force didn't care one way or another. To them it was just another case. But it seemed to me that Officers Jack Hardy, Jared Baker, Joe Denton, Lance Speer, and Nick Evans wanted the money and a whole lot more. It is my opinion that the five of them likely teamed up to circumvent their sergeants and destroy me and my reputation, but it would all collapse in due time.

After I was removed from my command, Hardy made an internal affairs complaint against me and claimed I tipped off the Faribault police chief and Rice County Sheriff about the wiretap investigation of the Tre-Tre Crips street gang without proper authorization. In legal terms, he claimed I made an unauthorized disclosure, but obviously nobody told him I was authorized to make the disclosure. Regardless, it was the foundation for the infamous "cover story."

On September 27, 2007, I received a phone call from attorney Fred Bruno. Bruno was an attorney cops turned to for legal advice when union attorneys had conflicts of interest or other issues. I had known Bruno for years, and I respected his advice, so I naturally consulted with him after I was removed from VOTF. Bruno told me that assistant US attorney Henry Stahl had called him and threatened to arrest me for "running [my] mouth about the public corruption case." Nothing could have been further from the truth. Stahl told Bruno, "I'm this close to having Keefe arrested." It seemed to me that Stahl was reckless and desperate, and he knew I hated him. We were polar opposites, and in my view, Stahl was unpredictable and dangerous from start to finish. I saw Stahl as a sinister man with a narcissist personality; he was one of the assistant US attorneys who claimed the public corruption case would be shut down if Jackson ever lied. But when Jackson lied, Stahl and his supervisors seemed to turn a blind eye. What really happened was that Deputy Chief Parker and Captain Henry Newton were talking about the case and somebody sent Stahl after me. I suspect it was Parker or VOTF officers. Parker later admitted during an unrelated lawsuit that he told the police union president and treasurer in the fall of 2007 about the public corruption case, which was supposed to be top secret. Furthermore, Newton was known for having a big mouth, and he accidentally spilled the beans at a staff meeting on July 9, 2007. Two months prior to that, he was overheard by homicide detectives telling a lieutenant about the public corruption case. Nevertheless, the bad cops, agents, and attorneys saw it as an opportunity to accuse me, and Stahl seemed happy to make the threat. Stahl and his supervisor's erratic behavior would only get worse as the criminal case against Officer Roberts moved closer to trial.

The VOTF officers knew I'd had run-ins with the ATF supervisors in the past, so they thought the MPD/ATF Faribault case with the Tre-Tre Crips, in which I'd had two disputes with the ATF, would fit as the cover story. But it all backfired after somebody in the FBI came forward and allegedly told Internal Affairs that the cover story was bogus, according to Internal Affairs sergeant Shaw.

Another dirty trick the FBI and MPD used was to claim I tipped off the black police officers about the public corruption case. That, too, fell apart, as two of the so-called corrupt black officers continued talking to Jackson after I allegedly "tipped them off." Obviously, if they had been tipped off, they would never have talked to or gone near Jackson. It was a relentless salvo of lies to get me removed from the task force so they could get their unrestricted overtime. Some officers were making well over $40,000 a year in overtime, according to Major Anna Wagner, before the FBI finally figured out they were the problem. It would only get worse as desperate cops, agents, and attorneys feared I would expose them in the pending Officer Roberts trial.

In fall 2007 I arranged a meeting with US Congressman Keith Ellison. I knew Ellison from previous district court encounters when I was a homicide detective, and Ellison was a well-known defense attorney. We had been adversaries, and we'd had cases together, but now I needed to let someone in power who understood law enforcement know what was going on and who was involved. Ellison warned me to be careful, and he made it clear to me that the feds would try to frame me if I continued to fight and expose FBI corruption. Ellison was spot-on correct.

VOTF officers took everything to another level a few months later, in December 2007, when another dubious informant—if not Jackson himself—gave VOTF officers deliberately false information. Only the culpable officers know the identity of the dubious "informant." Regardless, VOTF officers launched a raid on an innocent family's home on December 16 while they were all in bed, sleeping. It was an absolute assault on an innocent family. A mother, a father, and their six children ages 3-15 were sleeping in their home when task force cops used a SWAT team to carry out the raid just before 1:00 in the morning on December 16, 2007. When the SWAT team breached the door the homeowner woke up, grab his shotgun and fired off two rounds to scare off what he naturally assumed were intruders, and thats when two officers were shot from the spray of the shotgun pellets. Fortunately, neither officer, the homwowner, or his wife and kids were killed.

The first MPD press release came out approximately four hours after the assault at 5:02 a.m. on December 16, 2007, and said two officers had been shot by an adult male, but were not injured thanks to their helmets and bullet proof vests. Mayor Rybak and the city council were copied on the press release along with several commanders and city officials. However, the press release never mentioned the officers raided the wrong house. In fact, it implied the raid was justified and it said an adult male was taken into custody. The press release went further and said, "several officers returned fire, but no one in the house was injured." An innocent mother and father and their six little kids were literally attacked in the middle of the night and the press release said no one in the house was injured. The children's uncle told a Startribune reporter, "All these gunshots in the house. They don't know whats going on. Flying bullets in the house and they just cried." Needless to say, all of those children and their parents were traumatized, and sadly, they may have long term psychological damage. I suspect they would disagree no one in the house was "injured."

Very basic rudimentary checks that would have taken less than ten minutes would have revealed that they had the wrong address. After the raid and the address became public information, detectives throughout the city ran basic routine checks on the address, and every detective was able to very quickly confirm within a few minutes that VOTF had the wrong address. It was almost impossible for them to not see that they had the wrong address. Cops and detectives were shocked. Moreover, it was amazing that VOTF officers were able to get a judge to sign off on such a vague search warrant that authorized the SWAT team to execute a high-risk no-knock search warrant in the middle of the night and blow down the doors of an innocent family's home. It ended after a shootout with the homeowner. Remarkably, nobody was killed. The rumor around the department was that VOTF officers may have been chasing $200,000 in drug money to seize and put into their private overtime account. Seemingly, uncontrolled corruption and greed almost killed an innocent family and SWAT officers, and nobody was ever disciplined.

VOTF officers' sloppy high-risk search warrant for the wrong address clearly jeopardized the lives of fellow MPD officers on the SWAT team, and they were led there by a dubious informant. Was it Jackson? It was an informant, but who? I was on the record warning everyone about dubious informants, and now this fiasco had occurred. None of it would have happened if I had still been the VOTF commander.

Regardless of what VOTF officers and agents were doing, it had a chilling effect throughout the department. How was it even possible? What had the MPD become? First they removed me from VOTF, and now they were able to launch a high-risk raid on an innocent family's home with apparently no accountability. The raid fiasco went to a whole new level of potential misconduct, and to make matters worse, there was no legitimate internal accountability. The raid made it very clear to the rank and file that something was seriously wrong. It was obvious that some officers within the department had absolute impunity, but why? I believe the culpable VOTF officers should have been suspended and eventually terminated, but nothing happened. They were the same group of cops who had helped the FBI attack me, and everyone knew it. The MPD was literally out of control, but everyone kept quiet for fear of losing his or her job. It was clear to everyone that some VOTF officers were protected. They had immunity to do whatever they wanted.

The city quickly paid the family approximately $700,000, and nobody was ever held accountable for endangering the lives of the SWAT team and the innocent family. Police commanders and city leaders apparently never, to my knowledge, questioned a thing, or if they did, they took whatever they were told hook, line, and sinker. A legitimate Internal Affairs investigation would have resulted in several compelled and noncompelled statements, but none of that ever happened. Years later it was revealed that the officer who signed the warrant was new to the VOTF unit. That officer was a respected and honorable officer of the highest integrity. It was obvious to everyone who reviewed the warrant that veteran officers were likely behind this fiasco and that the officer in question was just used to sign the bad warrant. Several officers' lives were at risk, as were the lives of an innocent family, and there was absolutely no accountability whatsoever. None. The city had more important things to do, such as keeping me quiet.

CHAPTER 3
MEDIA ATTACK NUMBER 1

Media attack number one occurred on the evening of January 24, 2008. Local Fox News affiliate KMSP's reporter Tom Lyden launched what felt like a malicious character assassination. He based his story on the infamous cover story that claimed I had notified the Faribault Police Chief and Rice County Sheriff about a wiretap investigation in their jurisdiction without proper authorization. The story was all a bald-faced lie—absolute, 100 percent fake news! And to make matters worse, he claimed I had "jeopardized the lives of fellow officers." The story accused me of what VOTF officers had done a few weeks earlier. It was strict adherence to the mantra "Admit nothing, deny everything, and counteraccuse."

Lyden opened up the nine o'clock evening news standing in front of Minneapolis city hall with all the drama of a Broadway show and said, "Our top story, a Minneapolis cop accused tonight of leaking information that could jeopardize the lives of fellow officers." And with that bit of patently false information, the media and its cronies in the MPD, and perhaps the FBI, destroyed my career in just a few minutes. As sick and false as it was, it would only get worse. The people fighting me knew I could send them to prison for their criminal misconduct. They had no choice but to destroy me; there was no turning back.

At the time of the tv news story, I was the commander of the Third Precinct's property crimes division. I was a public employee working in a police precinct that was open 24-7. I had an office and was there every day during business hours. I had a public landline telephone and a city cell phone, but Lyden never stopped by the precinct and asked me about the horrible allegations. Lyden called my lawyer shortly before he went live with his story and gave him a heads up, but he never told him he was going to make outlandish accusations which I considered defamatory. Why didn't he come directly to me? I feel strongly that Lyden should be compelled to give up his sources.

The VOTF officers knew the raid was a reflection of their trickery and deceit, and they also knew I would eventually expose that as well as Jackson's apparent lies, so they presumably launched a preemptive strike and accused me of what they had done—jeopardizing the lives of fellow officers. It was all calculated deception designed to destroy me and my reputation before I went public and exposed them. Fear and paranoia seemingly drove them over the edge.

Years later, my attorneys and I discovered that VOTF officer Denton's name was on the MPD public information officer's log on January 24, 2008, next to "Tom Lyden, KMSP TV." Denton would later deny he was Lyden's source despite detailed phone records that seemed to show him calling Lyden on the day of the story. Denton wasn't the public information officer, so why was his name noted on the log next to Lyden's name?

A few weeks prior to this first media attack, I received a call from a number I recognized, but I didn't have a contact name associated it. I called the number back, and it was FBI supervisor Bryce Turner. Turner claimed he accidentally called me. Why did he even have my number? I deleted Turner's name and number as well as the name and number of every other FBI agent from my phone. I wanted nothing to do with the FBI agents. At the time, I thought Turner was calling because some black officers had sued the MPD and he may have been afraid the FBI secret of unjustly targeting black police officers would be exposed.

When Lyden made the claims about me he said something at the end of his report that really caught my attention. Lyden said, "Sources tell FOX 9 though that this is more than inside baseball that eventually it may connect up to that lawsuit involving four African American officers who are suing the MPD. I have a feeling we haven't heard the last of this." When Lyden said that, I immediately suspected Turner was one of Lyden's sources because of his phony call a few weeks earlier. I never talked to any of the four African American officers about their lawsuit. I didn't have any interest in it in any way, shape, or form. I absolutely did not care. It was none of my business, period. I clearly remember myself swearing out loud and calling out Turner's name repeatedly after the Lyden story. I was furious! I suspected Turner right away. Today I firmly believe Turner and Denton, and probably their superiors, were behind the story. Once again, paranoia likely sent the MPD and the FBI in the wrong direction, and it wouldn't be the last time.

The FBI put out an office alert on me the day after this media attack, but why? An office alert is to let agents know when someone unfriendly may be trying to make entry into the office. Did they put out the alert because they were behind the story? I never had any desire to ever go back to the Minneapolis FBI office. In fact, I refused, yet they put out the bogus office alert anyhow. What was the motive? Was it to give the appearance that the media attack was justified? No one knows for sure what they were up to, but the trail affirms potential collusion between the cops and the FBI, and the need for a full-scale criminal investigation. This media attack labeled me as unstable and potentially corrupt. It falsely claimed I endangered law enforcement officers' lives. It was patently false, and for a cop, the only thing worse was to be accused of murder. Lyden's story set the MPD on fire with wild rumors and accusations. It felt to me like absolute character assassination.

Turner and FBI agent David Krause called me a few times after I left VOTF, and Turner especially wanted me to come to his office and "talk." I would never work with an FBI supervisor who I heard arrogantly tell his agents during a staff meeting that he didn't want to do anything that was exculpatory. That was not the way we operated in Homicide. Besides, I didn't like him anyway. Turner asked me to have lunch one day, but I made up an excuse to avoid him. I had no time for him. I can't recall everything we talked about, but I'm pretty sure I made a counteroffer to have Turner come to the Homicide office. But Turner knew full well that everything in there was audio and video recorded, and he likely wanted nothing to do with any of that business.

Years later, during officer Denton's first deposition in state court, he denied ever giving the media any information about me, but when Denton was advised that my lawyers had cell phone records of his that showed several calls to reporters, he changed his answers and repeatedly claimed he could not remember or recall when he talked to reporters. Eventually, Denton was forced to admit he often talked to them, but he denied giving them any derogatory and false information about me. Denton had no business talking to any reporters in the first place. It wasn't his job. He wasn't the public relations officer, but I saw him as a very emotionally insecure man who desperately needed attention.

Four days after the first media attack, Minneapolis *Star Tribune* reporter David Chanen did a follow-up report to Lyden's story on January 28, 2008, and city cell phone records showed Chanen was in contact with Officer Denton, Deputy Chief Parker, and Captain Billy Wright on multiple occasions on January 27, 2008.

Media attack number one fortified the cover story that falsely claimed I had notified the Faribault chief and Rice County sheriff without proper authorization, and it went further with the bogus claim about jeopardizing fellow officers' lives. On the contrary, I put my career on the line to protect the lives of Faribault police officers, Rice County deputies, and Minnesota state troopers working in southern Minnesota. In reality, this attack felt to me like nothing but payback for not turning a blind eye to all the VOTF misconduct, and I feel strongly that the only way to get to the bottom of all this is a special prosecutor and a federal grand jury.

Remember my request that assistant US attorney Folk alert the Faribault police chief and Rice County sheriff that their officers were in danger of being shot and killed on traffic stops? This was now twisted to claim that I had compromised my own officers' and agents' safety by briefing the chief and sheriff about the threat to kill their officers on a future traffic stop. It was insane. Only a complete fool would buy into such lunacy. Folk knew it was silly, and he sided with me. The chief and sheriff needed to be briefed so they could warn their officers and deputies there was a credible threat to kill them on a future traffic stop. Nevertheless, the bad cops, and maybe FBI agents as well, flipped the script and claimed I endangered my own officers' and agents' lives when I notified the chief and sheriff, but they apparently did not know assistant US attorney Folk authorized me to make the initial disclosure. It was all a well-designed, calculated lie by the reporter's so-called sources, designed to destroy me because they feared I would eventually expose them in court for covering up evidence and overlooking Jackson's lies.

Seemingly, they were all scared to death I would expose them if I testified on behalf of Officer Roberts. Just the thought of me testifying for Roberts likely sent chills down the spine of every cop, agent, and attorney involved in their sleazy game of trickery and deceit. They had to destroy me because the truth could potentially put them all in prison.

In my mind, VOTF officers had compromised a family's safety and fellow officers' safety when they launched that reckless raid a month earlier in December 2007. On the contrary, I fought hard to protect the safety of Faribault police officers, Rice County deputies, and Minnesota state troopers by putting an end to a ridiculous nondisclosure clause that prohibited officers from knowing that gang members had made threats to kill them during a future traffic stop.

ATF agent Lawson argued that if the authorities in Faribault found out about their case, it would be compromised. He didn't trust the local authorities. I considered that ridiculous, and I felt Lawson was being unreasonable and irrational. As I saw it, the ATF case was just another run-of-the-mill gangbanger drugs-and-guns case, but it seemed that to Lawson it was the crime of the century.

Nevertheless, when the VOTF cops made up the infamous cover story, they did not know all the details. They thought their haphazard cover story would work. All they knew was that I, Pedowski, and Lawson had had a couple disagreements. They had no idea Folk gave me the green light to brief the chief and sheriff. The cops and FBI were in panic mode, trying to destroy my career. They had to have known that what they were doing was criminal and there was no turning back, so they had reporters put out the false stories, hoping I would back down. But it only motivated me more to expose them. However, it did cause me a phenomenal amount of stress. The thought of cops, and possibly FBI agents, using the media to attack me to try to make me back down was surreal. It was clear to me that the bad apples used my disagreements with two lower-level ATF supervisors as their cover story.

Another point to remember is that I denied ATF supervisor Samuel Lawson's request for around-the-clock coverage of the ongoing MPD/ATF wiretap. I had admonished Lawson that an undercover response to a 911-type call, such as a shooting, would endanger officers' and agents' lives. Was an ATF supervisor one of Lyden's sources? I think the ATF was used by the cops, but it doesn't preclude anyone in the ATF from stepping up to the plate and making false statements about me. I had knocked them down twice, and they may have wanted revenge.

When reporter Tom Lyden gave his report on the nine o'clock news, my wife crawled into the fetal position and cried. I was beyond livid. I would later tell my friends that if Lyden had knocked on my door that night, I would have shot him at point-blank range with a 12-gauge shotgun full of deer slugs. I wasn't serious, but I wanted that message to get back to the dirty cops, agents, and Lyden.

Understandably, being attacked by my commanders, the FBI, and attorneys caused me phenomenal stress. I could not sleep for more than a couple of hours a day. They took the corruption to a whole new level, and it was extremely dangerous. They were committed to keeping me quiet because they knew then, and still know today, that what they did likely warrants federal prison.

My friends convinced me not to carry my gun because they could see I was not myself. My friends knew some dirty cops and agents were framing me. They didn't know what was going on, but they knew it was big-time corruption. They also knew I would never stand for it, so I was a threat to the cops, agents, and attorneys if I exposed them. My life was on the line. It was obvious to real cops that the law enforcement officers behind those false news stories were criminals with badges and were dangerous and unpredictable. The dirty deed of taking stone-cold lies to the media to cover up criminal misconduct was a whole new level of deep-rooted corruption in Minneapolis.

Murdering a cop was not out of the question for the bad cops who wanted me silenced. My closest friends and fellow homicide detectives reminded me about the Minneapolis cop who was about to expose a burglary ring and was murdered. They reminded me of the Miami River cop murders. My friends cautioned me that if I was carrying a gun and the dirty cops and agents approached me, they could lie and say I was reaching for my gun and then legally kill me. This was advice I was getting from well-trained and experienced officers and homicide detectives who, like me, had a lot of experience investigating officer-involved shootings. It wasn't a stretch by any means. More concerning was that they had several drug-addicted informants who would do literally anything for a few bucks.

Unbeknownst to me, a few months later, Deputy Chief Parker was deposed in a civil lawsuit, and he admitted he told Minneapolis Police Union officials about the FBI's public corruption case in late summer 2007. In doing so, he unwittingly may have confessed to committing several crimes, but perhaps more importantly, he affirmed it was he himself who had spread the news throughout the department of an FBI probe into internal corruption. Union officers told me that Parker was telling people that I tipped off the black police officers. I felt it was a sick and calculated lie on the part of a high-ranking police commander. If it was true, and I believe it was, the Minneapolis deputy chief of police was literally trying to frame me for the crimes he himself had likely committed.

The day before Parker gave his deposition in the civil suit, MPD Internal Affairs sergeant Robert Krebs and Sergeant Dave Denno were removed from the internal affairs case I filed against VOTF officers after I was relieved of my command. My first internal affairs complaint was initially being investigated by Krebs, Denno, and Shaw. My understanding was that everything was turned over to rookie investigator Sgt. Shaw. This was very odd. Why would the department let a rookie investigator take over a major case of potential overtime fraud and corruption? In my mind, there could be only one reason—to protect the people I was exposing.

Krebs and Denno were honorable men. They would never cover up evidence, so they had to be replaced. Parker gave the order to get rid of them and replace them with Shaw. The MPD was boiling in corruption, and the water was rising.

CHAPTER 4
RICO CASE

On February 29, 2008, agent E. J. Wilkins of the Minneapolis FBI put out another office alert on me. This was now the second office alert in as many months. I had no contact with or interest in the FBI after I left VOTF, so why the alerts? I believe it was payback because I told Parker a few days earlier that the Minneapolis FBI was corrupt. The FBI placed a picture of my Minnesota driver's license inside the front door of their Minneapolis field office and said I was "precluded" from entering the FBI office. They added that should he be allowed in, agents were to use appropriate caution. This was just the beginning of the FBI's dirty tricks. The FBI was obsessed with me because they were afraid I would expose their alleged criminal misconduct.

MPD commanders were equally obsessed with me exposing everything, so on two separate occasions they ordered me to undergo the grueling Minnesota Multiphasic Personality Inventory (MMPI) psychological exam as a ruse to get rid of me with the expectation that it would find I was unfit for duty. The exams took hours. Parker and his friends were desperate. He knew how difficult those exams were, so they hoped I would fail, but it all backfired. Not only did I pass, but I scored far above average on ethics and integrity. The doctor told me he had no doubt everything I was saying was true, but he advised me to just forget about the corruption I was trying to expose and let it go. I told him that wasn't an option. The doctor told me he could not let me go back to work as 100 percent conditionally fit unless I agreed to let it go. I said to him, "Do what ya gotta do, doc; I'm not letting it go. They are bad cops and I'm going after them." The doctor shook his head and allowed me to return to work as conditionally fit. He wouldn't give me a 100 percent conditionally fit pass because I refused to back down. I didn't care. I was going back to work, and there was nothing the doctor could do.

On June 23, 2008, I was ordered into Internal Affairs as a witness in another officer's case. This was weird. It was a compelled Garrity statement, which meant I had no choice. If I failed to show up or answer any questions, I would be fired immediately. The Internal Affairs investigator was Sgt. Shaw. Knowing Shaw was assigned to my first Internal Affairs complaint against VOTF officers, I was immediately suspicious. Near the end of the interview, I was asked whether I had taped Jackson during his interview at the FBI safe house. What did that have to do with allegedly being a witness to another officer's potential misconduct during a taped telephone call? Everything was on the tape; what more could I offer? Absolutely nothing. It all felt like a ruse to see whether I had a tape from when I interviewed Jackson in 2007 at the FBI safe house. And it went further. At the end of the interview in this other officer's misconduct case, Sgt. Shaw also wanted to know whether I taped any of the Monday-morning meetings at the Minneapolis FBI office regarding the Jackson case. It was during those meetings that assistant US attorneys warned everyone that if Jackson lied, the public corruption case would end immediately.

This act of using MPD Internal Affairs to elicit information to determine whether I had tangible evidence (a tape) that they were covering up evidence (Jackson's lies and assistant US attorneys' warnings) was, I believe, a classic Title 18 Conspiracy to Obstruct Justice case, and perhaps a RICO case. A month after I was interviewed as a witness and confirmed I did not have a tape of Jackson's bogus stories or any tapes of assistant US attorneys' warnings during Monday-morning meetings at the FBI office, Officer Roberts was indicted for accepting a bribe.

The million-dollar question is, Which attorney or attorneys coached the Internal Affairs investigator, Sgt. Shaw, to ask me whether I had a tape of my interview with Jackson or the FBI meetings? I believe that

Roberts would never have been indicted if I had a tape of Jackson's bogus stories or of assistant US attorneys warning that the case would immediately cease if Jackson lied. Assistant US Attorneys could not indict Roberts until those questions were answered, so somebody made the decision to use MPD Internal Affairs under the guise of a routine Internal Affairs investigation to get the answer. Collusion? Calling me in to Internal Affairs as a witness in another officer's case and then asking me whether I had a tape of Jackson or FBI meetings was classic pretext and a whole lot more. It is arguably the foundation of a RICO case.

Many attorneys might argue that cops and government agents using the arm of a government agency to further their criminal misconduct is hands-down a RICO case. Attorneys and I believe that assistant US attorneys could not indict Roberts until they knew I did not have a tape of Jackson telling conflicting stories during his interview at the FBI safe house. They also had to know whether there were any tapes of the Monday-morning FBI office meetings warning cops and agents the case would end immediately if Jackson lied. Officers and agents were told multiple times that if Jackson lied, he would be sent back to prison and the deal was void. I was in the homicide unit before I became the VOTF commander, and everything I did with witnesses and everyone else was either audio or video recorded, and that past practice of transparency alarmed everyone who was "rolling dirty."

I had been vocal about the veracity of Jackson's allegations, and it scared the FBI and US attorneys. So they did the unthinkable; they quite possibly violated the RICO Act. They seemingly went over the cliff, and there was no turning back. The act of using Minneapolis Police Internal Affairs to determine whether I had evidence that they were covering up evidence of Jackson telling lies to save himself from prison took this entire case to a level not, I believe, seen before in the history of the FBI or Department of Justice. For the first time in the history of the United States, US attorneys may have been using a local police department's internal affairs unit to ascertain whether a high-ranking cop had evidence of FBI agents and assistant US attorneys covering up evidence—namely, Jackson's apparent lies. This act is so egregious it is literally unbelievable. The powers that be were literally out of control with fear and paranoia.

This is very important, so it needs to be summarized again. On June 23, 2008, I was called into Internal Affairs as a witness in the Internal Affairs case of another officer (Captain Delvin Crawford). This is where the Minneapolis US attorney's office seemingly turned this entire case upside down. In no uncertain terms, if they did it, they made it a potential RICO case. RICO was designed to take down the mafia and organized crime, and fortunately it doesn't exclude corrupt law enforcement officers. I believe that the US attorneys and the FBI were scared to death that I had a tape of my July 25, 2007, interview with Jackson or tapes of the Monday-morning meetings at the Minneapolis FBI office. If I had a tape, or tapes, and they indicted Roberts, I could show up in court with a tape or produce a tape after Roberts was charged, and it would literally bring down the house.

Assistant US attorneys had gone on the record stating that if Jackson lied about anything, the case would end and he would be sent back to prison. I was on the record telling the MPD that I believed Jackson was a calculated liar. The risk was way too high for the feds to indict Roberts and then have me produce a tape. It would destroy their careers and most likely result in termination coupled with disbarment and criminal charges. The feds needed to find out somehow if I had a tape of Jackson changing his story regarding officers whom he alleged were corrupt, and FBI meetings, and they did not want to use the legitimate tools of the trade to call me into court. If they called me into a court hearing before trial, I would expose everyone and everything to a judge who would immediately shield me from future persecution. They could not risk it, because if I did have a tape, their careers were over. They had no choice but to dig a deeper hole.

The feds knew they had no choice but to team up with the MPD and somehow surreptitiously find out whether I had a tape of Jackson's unfounded stories or whether I taped the FBI meetings which assistant US attorneys attended. So they turned to their friends in VOTF, and VOTF officers turned to their friend in Internal Affairs, Sgt. Shaw.

That is why Captain Kay Robinson's February 2008 order putting Shaw in charge of my first Internal Affairs complaint is so damaging. Robinson did not just sign that order; she signed it for Deputy Chief Parker, and she smartly noted it. I don't think she knew everything that was going on, but she knew removing two highly respected Internal Affairs sergeants from the biggest case of police corruption in the history of the MPD and the state of Minnesota and beyond was something she wanted nothing to do with, so she made sure she properly signed her name, but per Deputy Chief Parker.

The cops, attorneys, and perhaps FBI agents laid the framework for a potential RICO case. The actions of the culpable attorneys and everyone who helped them were under the color of law. They used their power and authority to destroy me, and along the way they may have committed several crimes. The penalties for this abuse of power are severe and far ranging, which is another reason why the FBI is still to this day literally scared to open this case and do its job; they know it could lead to multiple indictments.

On June 23, 2008 after the MPD had Shaw firmly in control of all the internal affairs cases surrounding VOTF corruption (Krebs and Denno had been removed in February), Stahl—or somebody—made his move with the help of VOTF and Shaw and ordered me into Internal Affairs under an apparently false pretense. It would appear as though Stahl, Shaw, VOTF officers, and maybe the FBI and the Minneapolis City Attorney's Office put all their cards on the table and rolled the dice. It's impossible to know what they were all thinking, but make no mistake about it: whoever was involved collectively conspired to work as a team and vigorously pursue a black police officer and anyone who got in their way. Yes, Officer Roberts was found guilty of accepting a bribe, but the seeming criminal misconduct of those involved to secure his conviction makes his $200 bribe look like a two-year-old stealing candy.

Retired FBI agent Dan Vogel provided me with a written account of some of the FBI misconduct in this case, but he wasn't privy to everything. Nonetheless, Vogel has studied a lot of police and FBI corruption around the country, and with the exception of the New York Mafia murders under FBI agent Lin DeVecchio and New York mobster Greg Scarpa, and the Boston murders under FBI agent John Connolly and Whitey Bulger, this case is right there with them—and perhaps even bigger on a sophistication scale. Never before in the history of our country has a major metropolitan police department allegedly conspired with assistant US attorneys to direct a case—and a racially motivated one, no less. The bigger question is whether the FBI was involved in using MPD Internal Affairs to go fishing for a tape of exculpatory evidence. The FBI had miscarried in this case, but were they now helping assistant US attorneys take this to a higher level? Were Minneapolis assistant city attorneys involved as well?

The June 23 order mandating me into Internal Affairs to give a compelled witness statement in a case involving Capt. Crawford was apparently drafted under the leadership of an attorney, or attorneys. Crawford was a captain and was one of the cops Jackson claimed was on the take, but that was just another spontaneous lie by Jackson. Crawford and Jackson went to college together. Jackson said Crawford was on the take, and he also said Crawford was from Chicago. Crawford was actually from Cleveland. True to form, Jackson couldn't keep his lies straight when he talked about Crawford and every other cop.

During the initial stages of the public corruption investigation, Jackson made a call to Crawford and asked him to run a license plate after Jackson claimed he was having trouble with somebody. The call was taped, and I was called into Internal Affairs as a witness. It was likely a pretext. How can anyone be a witness to something that's on tape? It was reckless and stupid.

Of course, we've already seen that the real reason I was called in as a witness was because the US attorney's office was apparently afraid that I had taped Jackson on July 25, 2007, when I interviewed him at the FBI safe house. They were also afraid I taped FBI meetings with assistant US attorneys, warning everyone the case would be shut down if Jackson lied. If assistant US attorneys indicted Roberts and I exposed Jackson's lies on tape later, the attorney's career was over and, so was everyone else's career up the chain of command. So they needed to find out if I had a tape recording of that interview or any FBI meetings.

At the end of the interview Shaw looked intently at her notes and asked me if I was in possession of any physical evidence as part of the investigation against Capt. Crawford? I replied, "No." Shaw then asked me if I taped any FBI meetings? Again I replied, "No." Shaw continued to persist and said, "You have no recordings of those meetings?" I replied, "None." Shaw then asked me if I taped any of Jackson's statements, and again I replied, "No." And with that volley of questions I believe Shaw locked herself and her partners into the middle of a massive case of criminal misconduct. I BELIEVE THIS IS THE CRUX OF A TITLE 18 CONSPIRACY TO OBSTRUCT JUSTICE CASE, AND PERHAPS A RICO CASE.

Shaw went head first over the cliff. I was called into Internal Affairs as a "witness" and she asked me at least four different times if I had any tape recordings. It was absolute pretext in my mind. Total fraud. The definition of pretext is a reason given in justification of a course of action that is not the real reason. The real reason I believe was she wanted to know if I had any tape recordings of Jackson lying when I interviewed him at the FBI safe house, or assistant US attorneys warning everyone during FBI meetings that if Jackson lied the case would end immediately.

I believe it was a very calculated group effort on the part of MPD officers and federal agents fishing for evidence to see if I had evidence in the form of audio tapes that they were covering up Jackson's alleged lies which in legal terms is called exculpatory evidence. And they used the strong arm of MPD Internal Affairs to get the job done by demanding I give them a compelled statement that would have resulted in my termination if I did not cooperate.

It was a desperate move by cops, agents, and attorneys who were seemingly abusing their power and authority under the color of law to create an "official investigation." Moreover, it affirmed potential collusion and conspiracy on the part of the involved players, and criminal defense attorneys believe this act of detailed conspiracy made it a potential RICO case. That is some serious business. The RICO Act gives the government a great deal of power, but the problem in this case is that the government agents are the suspects. The cops, agents, and attorneys are all suspects. A month after I confirmed in June 2008 that I did not have any tapes, Officer Roberts was indicted.

In July of 2008, I sent out a citywide email seeking officers to work off duty at Wells Fargo banks. I was the supervisor for all the officers who worked off duty at Wells Fargo. Generally there were around eighty officers who worked for the bank. A month later, on August 28, 2008, Lieutenant Brian Schafer, the supervisor for off-duty officers at the Minneapolis Public Schools, sent out a similar email to officers who worked off duty. Shortly after I sent my email, I was written up for improper use of the city email system. The emails Schafer and I sent were common practice, as this off-duty work benefited the city and the police department. Needless to say, Lt. Schafer was never written up for his email.

The MPD made it clear to me they were out to get me in any way they could.

On August 17, I briefed Hennepin County Sheriff Rich Stanek on the apparent corruption, and we agreed, based on the advice of Attorney Fred Bruno, not to do anything until after Roberts's trial.

Bruno gave me the okay to brief Stanek as long as he agreed to keep the conversation and a detailed fifteen-page letter summarizing the corruption confidential. I wanted to brief someone in law enforcement outside the MPD, and Stanek seemed like a logical choice. He was a former Minneapolis police captain, and I had worked with him in the past. I felt it was important for an independent law enforcement agency to have knowledge of the alleged corruption involving Minneapolis police officers and FBI agents. I had already briefed Congressman Ellison, but now it was time to bring on a local law enforcement officer with power and authority to act, if need be.

Sheriff Stanek immediately agreed to keep everything confidential, and nobody except me and Attorney Fred Bruno was aware of the letter. Bruno didn't want anything in my letter revealed to anyone until after Roberts's trial. Bruno was concerned that if the information in the letter got out, the feds would try to claim I somehow obstructed their bogus case. Stanek was in agreement; the letter and its contents needed to remain confidential. Bruno and I have no doubt Sheriff Stanek honored the agreement.

On October 28, the Minneapolis FBI supervisor special agent (SSA), Kevin Irving, responded to a letter from Shaw, who seemed to be desperately trying to frame me. Shaw was seeking evidence from the FBI that I had miscarried and was "banned" from the FBI office. Irving claimed they had no such evidence because I was never "banned" from the FBI office. Irving said my security clearance wasn't renewed because I was reassigned to another unit within the MPD. This was true, but only because Irving and his agents and Minneapolis VOTF officers were seemingly going after black cops without any just probable cause and I refused to be part of their sinister plan.

FBI SSA Irving was clearly playing a semantics game with Shaw at this point, but why? Was the FBI trying to distance itself from the impending train wreck, or were they simply trying to sever their link with MPD? The FBI had plenty of lawyers to advise their agents about the dangers of a future civil suit, and by now they likely sensed future litigation against the city of Minneapolis, and perhaps the bureau as well. I wasn't backing down, so maybe it was time to play games with Shaw. Shaw didn't know it, but whatever relationship she'd had with the FBI, it was likely over now.

CHAPTER 5
FBI

IN EARLY 2009, ANXIETY GOT THE BEST OF MPD COMMANDERS AND the FBI. The Roberts trial was rapidly approaching, and they seemed scared to death that I would testify and expose everything. They knew I did not have a tape of Jackson's wild stories or any assistant US attorney warnings, but it obviously was not enough to put them at ease. A high-ranking officer exposing a massive case of corruption had them on their heels, and as the trial got closer, their anxiety grew more intense.

In February, Capt. Wright sent an email to Parker letting him know that reporter Paul McEnroe was seeking quotes from VOTF. Wright said, "I sense the truth has little to do with his story. It does bring up concerns that people have." So there you had the current criminal investigations division (CID) commander letting a deputy chief of police know that some VOTF officers were concerned about the pending *Star Tribune* story as well. Why would they care if they hadn't done anything wrong?

Parker sent a return email to Wright that stated, "They are in good hands with you, and you are with me." Parker and Wright were talking about VOTF officers and their concerns about the threat I was posing by exposing them. In other words, no worries. I've got your back. In that same email exchange Parker asked Wright if it was okay if some VOTF awards would be 2009 awards as opposed to 2008. What was going on here? **A deputy chief of police was asking a captain for permission?**

A few weeks later, Parker sent out a citywide email warning the rank and file that the media was preparing a story that would not look favorably upon the MPD. He advised everyone to remember that the media seldom puts out the full story, and that unfortunately the law precluded him from commenting. Right. Parker may have been scared to death the *Star Tribune* reporters were going to expose him and the feds, and he had it in his head that I was talking to the media. Little did he know that Attorney Fred Bruno and I were sitting back waiting for the right moment to expose Parker and his friends to the Department of Justice inspector general. Apparently Parker thought that just because he allegedly talked to the media about this case, so would I. He was dead wrong. *Star Tribune* reporter Paul McEnroe and I talked years later after I finally agreed to meet McEnroe at an Irish bar in Northeast Minneapolis. McEnroe told me that Parker was convinced I had been talking to him, and we had a good laugh over it. Paranoia makes your mind play tricks on you.

I tried bluffing McEnroe into admitting he was an FBI informant, but McEnroe denied it. But McEnroe always had information other reporters didn't have. At the very least, I have no doubt McEnroe was the FBI's go-to guy to put a good spin on stories they wanted out.

In March the MPD public information officer, Sergeant Marty Palmer, put out a citywide email to the rank and file regarding the upcoming *Star Tribune* news story. The MPD was giving the rank and file a subtle warning that talking to the media was a violation of department policy. (A few years later, Capt. Reed enhanced this policy because he, too, was apparently afraid I would expose MPD corruption.)

A few weeks later, in April, Parker once again sent out another email warning the troops not to believe what they read and heard from the local media. This time it was under the guise of a rah-rah letter with all his alleged favorable statistics. But he couldn't help taking a shot at attorneys and others he described as "naysayers" who routinely made "false accusations," and he noted that "tabloid journalism" was alive and well. Parker was setting the stage for what he thought would be doomsday, and if I had been talking to the media, it would have been.

Prior to Parker's email campaign, his apparent paranoia caused him to reach out to a Minneapolis Police Union officer who had some limited knowledge of Roberts's case. Parker was unaware that the officer and I had a good relationship, and the officer let me know that on two separate occasions in early 2009, Parker asked him whether I was going to testify in Roberts's trial. The first time Parker asked was on January 10, and the second time was on January 27. Why would Parker care if he hadn't done anything wrong? I testified in murder trials, rape trials, robbery trials, burglary trials, property crime trials, and traffic cases, and nobody in the MPD, especially a deputy police chief, ever asked or showed any concern. As a homicide detective, I was involved in some high-profile murder and gun cases, and I had the landmark federal case *United States v. Wright,* Yet all of a sudden a deputy Minneapolis chief of police was worried about whether I would testify in an upcoming trial?

In late April 2009, Parker tried to put a bright light on a four-page story *Star Tribune* reporters Paul McEnroe and Tony Kennedy ran about me and VOTF. Parker had to be so relieved the real corruption story was never told, so now it was time to put out a phony letter. Basically it was hugs and kisses to everyone.

Prior to the *Star Tribune*'s four-page story, Parker was convinced I had exposed him to the reporters. All those warnings and likely sleepless nights because he was afraid I had exposed him and his friends. All that energy was spent on nothing, but he wasn't out of the woods yet. The Roberts trial was only days away, and Parker had other problems. Many in the rank and file now hated him and the entire police administration for using what they perceived to be unethical VOTF cops to help them and the FBI charge a cop, and to make matters worse, I was served with the first of two subpoenas ordering me to testify in Roberts's case. Years later I would learn that the arrivals of those subpoenas were the talk of the town within the MPD and FBI.

Nevertheless, Parker made at least four key points in his April 2009 propaganda letter which could come back to haunt him:

1. "We will vigorously investigate any and all allegations of corruption. There is no acceptable degree of corruption in law enforcement."

2. "I brought the case to the FBI because I felt it was important to have an independent investigation of the allegations."
3. "I do want to publicly commend the officers who assisted the FBI in this investigation. In reality, there were only two officers assisting—not the whole Violent Offender Task Force stated in articles."
4. "We have the most transparent and accountable law enforcement agency in the region ..."

In my opinion, all four points were bald-faced lies.

After the four-part *Star Tribune* series became public, attorney Fred Bruno gave me the green light to notify the US Department of Justice's inspector general field office in Chicago. So on the afternoon of April 22, 2009 I called the Chicago field office and turned in MPD officers, FBI agents, and assistant US attorneys during a lengthy phone call to Inspector General Agent Vincent Schwartz. I let Schwartz know I would be following up with a detailed letter and a copy of my August 2008 letter to Sheriff Stanek. I was now on the record fighting back. I was going after the FBI, MPD, the Minneapolis US attorney's office, and the Minneapolis city attorney's office. It was the start of a real-world David and Goliath battle.

Five days later, on April 27, 2009, I sent a very detailed five-page letter to Inspector General Agent Norbert Flynn, and I included a copy of my letter to Sheriff Stanek. Those two letters alleged a phenomenal amount of potential criminal misconduct on the part of cops, FBI agents, and assistant US attorneys, which clearly meant this was a criminal case for FBI Inspections in Washington, DC.

Local FBI offices handle internal administrative problems with agents, but criminal misconduct is handled by FBI Inspections in Washington. I felt that my complaint should have gone there immediately, but that did not happen. Somehow somebody screwed up and sent my complaint up to the Minneapolis FBI field office. This was a major blunder. All the evidence was sent to the accused suspects. Was it really an accident, or was it deliberate? We may never know, but when that evidence arrived at the Minneapolis FBI field office, the FBI SSA, Kevin Irving, had an absolute legal and ethical responsibility to immediately secure everything and send it to Washington DC. But apparently he didn't. Instead he sent me a letter on May 1 seeking a meeting. What in the world was an accused suspect in an alleged corruption case I just exposed doing sending me a letter seeking a meeting?

I received the letter sometime between May 4 and May 6. Obviously I declined to talk to Irving. Instead I called the Chicago field office of the inspector general and demanded to know what was going on. The inspector general apologized to me for the screwup, but the bigger question was that of whether Agent Irving tipped off any fellow agents or attorneys in the Minneapolis FBI field office. If he had, he may have crossed a number of lines, many of which are potentially criminal. I made my complaint with the Chicago office of the inspector general because I didn't trust Irving or anyone in the Minneapolis FBI field office. Now at least one of the suspects, a very high ranking Minneapolis FBI agent, had confidential information that he could use to defend himself in the future. Needless to say, it jeopardized everything.

The mere fact that Irving was seeking a meeting was a huge red flag to me. Irving was a career FBI agent, and in my opinion he had no business sending me a letter seeking a meeting when everything I alleged was clearly criminal. It was obviously a case for FBI Inspections in Washington, DC. What was he really trying to do? Regardless of what he was trying to do, I felt it was an old-fashioned case of dirty pool no matter how you cut it. With the help of Fred Bruno, I had patiently waited to blow the whistle, and then the inspector general "accidentally" tipped off the suspects? We will probably never know whether it was intentional, but what we do know is that the FBI wasn't playing by the rules, and retired FBI agent Dan Vogel confirmed this in his summary of the Minneapolis field office.

U.S. Department of Justice

Federal Bureau of Investigation

In Reply, Please Refer to
File No.

111 Washington Avenue South
Suite 1100
Minneapolis, Minnesota 55401
May 1, 2009

Lieutenant Michael Keefe
Minneapolis Police Department
350 South Fifth Street
Room 130
Minneapolis, MN 55415-1389

Re: Corruption allegations

Dear Lt. Keefe:

    The Minneapolis Division of the FBI has become aware of allegations which have been levied by you against ▓▓▓▓▓ ▓▓▓▓▓▓▓▓▓▓▓▓▓▓▓▓▓▓▓▓▓▓▓▓▓ in the Minneapolis Division. In keeping with the FBI's strict standards of professional responsibility, you are requested to contact ▓▓▓▓▓ ▓▓▓▓▓▓▓▓▓▓▓▓▓▓▓▓▓ in order to more fully explore these allegations.

    If you have any questions or concerns regarding this matter, please contact ▓▓▓▓▓▓▓▓▓▓▓▓▓▓▓▓▓▓.

Sincerely,

cc: ▓▓▓▓▓▓▓▓▓▓▓

(FBI letter to Keefe for meeting, May 1, 2009)

On April 22, 2009, I received my first subpoena from Officer Roberts's attorney, Clayton Tyler, to testify on his client's behalf. A week later, on April 30, I received a second subpoena duces tecum to testify and to submit all applicable writings and documents related to the case. In short, if I had a tape or any other evidence, I was to bring it with me. By now the MPD and FBI knew there was no tape or other documented evidence, because they had already compelled me into Internal Affairs under false pretense searching for evidence. Sending me the subpoenas was just a routine inquiry for attorney Tyler, but it scared the feds and the MPD command staff. Years later I would find out that Tyler had been warning the city for a long time that he would be sending me a subpoena duces tecum to testify. In hindsight, it may have been what provoked them to order me into Internal Affairs under seemingly false pretenses and to commit several potential crimes along the way. Both subpoenas were sent to me via Minneapolis assistant city attorney Patrick O'Leary.

I have no doubt O'Leary immediately notified the MPD command staff and the FBI. The documents invariably sent shock waves throughout the MPD, FBI, and US attorney's office. Their worst nightmare had come true, and they did not know which way to turn. At the time, I was the Third Precinct Property Crimes commander, and during a precinct staff meeting on or about May 4, 2009, the Third Precinct inspector, Lucy Gerold, asked me what was going on in VOTF. She was referring to the recent *Star Tribune* series. She thought I could shed some light on the matter that had everyone upset, because I was the former VOTF commander.

I told her that I was aware of serious misconduct on the part of a few officers who were supposed to have helped the FBI uncover corruption, and that it was my opinion that some of them could eventually end up being indicted. She asked for my opinion, and I gave it to her. That's what you do when your boss asks for your opinion—no lies, nothing made up, just your straight-up opinion. It was my opinion in 2009 and it's my opinion today.

My staff meeting comments got back to Sgt. Shaw, so she called me about a voicemail I left her a few days earlier. Then she segued into the staff meeting comments, which I repeated to her. Shaw then took her alleged corruption to a new level. She sent a letter to Major Anna Wagner two days later, on May 6, and claimed I said officers and agents *were* being indicted, not *could* be. Shaw misrepresented what I had said, but why? She knew Parker and VOTF were on a sinking ship. Most likely she wanted to impress her superiors, whom she knew wanted to stop me, so she embellished her memo to please Maj. Wagner and Deputy Chief Parker.

Shaw went even further and claimed I said there were "sealed indictments" on the desk of Sheriff Stanek. Only an inexperienced investigator like Shaw could come up with something so stupid. She obviously had no idea what a sealed indictment was, and yet she was now claiming I said they were on the desk of Hennepin County sheriff Rich Stanek. How could a sealed indictment be on the desk of a county sheriff? It was ridiculous, but every commander in the incompetent, dysfunctional, and immoral MPD believed it because they, like Shaw, had virtually no investigative experience. If there were any sealed indictments for the arrest of cops and federal agents, they would be on the desk of a US attorney or the US marshal for the applicable jurisdiction, not the county sheriff.

Shaw changed her sealed indictment story by stating that "indictments were ready to go" by the time she wrote her bogus memo to Wagner two days later. Regardless, I believed Shaw had now literally manufactured evidence with her letter to Wagner. She later claimed she had a tape of her conversation with me, but when she was confronted about it by Internal Affairs investigator Sergeant Nolan Zabel, she said that the tape "malfunctioned." No such tape was ever produced.

If the tape had malfunctioned, Shaw should have sent it to the crime lab, but she didn't—because there was no tape. Ironically, during her deposition two years later, Shaw initially told me and my attorneys she never tape-recorded the call because she used her cell phone. Attorney Albert Goins pounced on that and demanded Shaw pick which story she was going with—the "tape malfunctioned" story she told Sgt. Zabel, or her latest claim that she used her cell phone? Shaw, with her upper lip trembling, and in a parched voice, decided she would stick with the original story she told Zabel.

At any rate, during the May 4, 2009, phone call, Shaw apparently panicked when I told her I spilled the beans to the Justice Department. Shaw most likely went into a complete frenzy, and I laid it on thick and really stuck it to Shaw because I believed she was working with the bad cops. I was on the offensive, and not only did Shaw panic, but they all seemed to panic. Within a few days after Shaw's phone call story, FBI SSA Irving and MPD deputy chief Parker carried out a number of attacks under the color of law. Shaw pumped them up, and they jumped on me like rabid animals. After Shaw wrote her letter to Wagner, she met with FBI agent David Krause and relayed her phone call story to him as well. Krause apparently relayed it up the FBI chain of command to Irving. In my mind, Shaw intentionally baited the MPD and the FBI because she knew they were looking for an excuse to destroy me, so she gave them just what they wanted. They seem to have never vetted a thing Shaw said, because they didn't care. I turned them in to the Justice Department; they were in power, and it was time to get even. The first thing the MPD and FBI commanders should have done was demand the tape Shaw claimed to have and listen to it. They had shown an overwhelming obsession with the possibility that I had a tape of them, or tapes of them, but now apparently they were not concerned about whether anything I had said about them was on tape.

The MPD and FBI were out of control, and it was about to get worse.

CHAPTER 6
MEDIA ATTACK NUMBER 2

WITH OFFICER ROBERTS'S TRIAL RAPIDLY APPROACHING, PARKER, THE FBI, and the US attorney's office were in full-blown panic mode. Assistant US Attorney Jay Schultz called Attorney Fred Bruno and, I felt, threatened me on May 5, 2009. It was unbelievable and beyond disgusting. Schultz told Bruno that if I took the stand he was really gonna go after me. So apparently this is what the US Justice Department does when they find out a cop will expose corruption involving fellow officers, federal agents, and attorneys. The trial had yet to begin, and the US government had already used seeming threats and intimidation to deter me and chill me from testifying, and it very quickly got much worse.

On May 6, the FBI sent out another crazy office alert on me after I refused to meet with agent Irving. This was now their third office alert. The alert was sent out by FBI agent B. Peterson, who claimed I was "Prohibited from FBI Minneapolis space" and further stated, "This is a personnel safety matter." Wow! All of a sudden, because I refused to talk to one of the highest-ranking FBI agents in Minneapolis, I was now somehow a threat to every Minneapolis FBI agent? What kind of dirty game was this? In big, bold letters, the alert said, "PROCEED WITH CAUTION."

A few days prior, I had been invited to meet with Minneapolis FBI SSA Irving, and now I was prohibited from the Minneapolis FBI office. What had changed? Nothing, except that I refused to meet with FBI SSA

Irving and the FBI knew I had turned them in to the US Department of Justice inspector general's Chicago field office. They were afraid I was on the verge of exposing everything during Officer Roberts's trial.

I never gave anyone from the FBI any indication I would ever go anywhere near the FBI office, so what kind of a dirty, corrupt game was this? Or were they just being childish? It was their third childish "office alert." The FBI was obsessed with me. If anything, the FBI was a threat to me and my family.

This was now the third time the FBI put out a bogus alert on me, but this time it was potentially criminal misconduct. The FBI sent out that third alert without an ounce of justification just before Roberts's trial, knowing full well I was a subpoenaed witness. Several prominent criminal defense attorneys believe this could be seen as potential witness tampering and obstruction of justice. The FBI may have crossed a number of ethical and criminal boundaries when they put out the third bogus alert on the eve of the Roberts trial. The FBI was digging a deeper hole in a feeble attempt to intimidate me.

After the FBI played their hand, it was time for Parker to play his hand. He did what was without a doubt one of the sleaziest and most rotten things any police commander could ever do. The first thing he did was relieve me of duty on May 8, 2009, under the pretext that I was spreading rumors. Parker seemed more than willing to latch onto Shaw's patently false claim that I was claiming officers were being indicted. Parker was a cop with years of experience, and yet he claimed to have bought into Shaw's lie, which was literally not even possible. And Parker should have known it.

Parker was livid. He, like FBI agent Irving, knew at this point that I had turned them in to the inspector general, and it was quite obvious to all of them that I, with the help of the inspector general, was moving to have them indicted for what I and my attorneys perceived to be multiple crimes. Parker was beside himself. He went even further, on May 8, and ordered the mayor's driver and bodyguard, Officer Grady Loftus, to go around city hall and show my Minnesota driver's license picture to all the city council members and tell them to be on the lookout for me and to consider me dangerous! It was absolutely unreal. All because I turned him and his friends in to the Department of Justice inspector general and he was afraid I would testify in Roberts's trial and expose everything. How did that make me dangerous or a threat to anyone? Obviously, it didn't. Parker and his friends dug a deep hole, but they were in power, and nobody could stop them for now.

Officer Loftus was a good man and just did what he was ordered to do. When my attorneys deposed him, he laid it all out. He told the attorneys that Parker's lackey, Maj. Wagner, gave him his marching orders to go around to all of the members of the city council, and show them my picture and explain the warning. What had I done to deserve something so hate filled and malicious? Nothing, but one thing was very clear to me: the people I was fighting were dangerous and desperate.

I really wanted to testify in Roberts's trial, but Attorney Fred Bruno would not allow me to do so, because he suspected the FBI and US attorney would set a perjury trap and falsely accuse me. All I had to do was truthfully answer one question that the feds knew their agents would claim was not true, and it would be my word against theirs. They would then charge me with perjury. In other words, if I stepped up and testified, they would likely frame me for telling the truth. It was all about self-preservation and covering the tracks of potential criminal misconduct. It was the US government at its worst. The powers that be seemed to have become the criminals.

Attorneys who have reviewed this case believe strongly that these alleged criminal acts on the part of the involved cops, agents, and attorneys to chill me and deter me from testifying are very serious. But when I didn't think it could get any more disgusting, Parker and his cronies took it to another level. They had already inflicted an enormous amount of damage. They had destroyed my career and reputation, but now they decided to put the icing on the cake and once again use the media to launch their second character-assassination attack. This time they used *Star Tribune* writer David Chanen, but as before, they got sloppy. They used their city cell phones to call in the attack, and they did it while Chanen was sitting at his desk writing the story on May

8, 2009. The cell phone evidence is overwhelming and irrefutable. No jury in the world would ever discount such evidence. In my opinion, Chanen was every bit as ruthless as Lyden, and both of these reporters either knowingly or unwittingly helped corrupt law enforcement officers further their attacks. That may allow the Justice Department, under the 1972 case *Branzburg v. Hayes*, to compel the reporters to give up their sources. These were not good people, or good cops calling up a reporter and exposing something for which the shield law was intended. These were law enforcement officers acting under the color of law, using the media to further alleged criminal misconduct. They seemingly used the media and MPD Internal Affairs to further their alleged crimes. Their goal was a success, because I never testified and all the dirty deeds of the MPD, the FBI, and the US attorney's office were never exposed. I was relieved of duty for allegedly being "disruptive" when I told Shaw officers could be indicted. Parker had no justification for relieving me of duty, and Roberts was found guilty of bribery.

Minneapolis was operating like an independent state free of the 1964 Civil Rights Act, and the worst was yet to come.

The allegedly corrupt officers, and maybe the FBI as well, seem to have made sure the *Star Tribune* blasted me out of the water. There was no way they were going to let me take the stand unblemished. The goal seemed to be to destroy my reputation so I could not be a credible witness, and Chanen's article did just that by painting me as an unhinged lunatic. The dirty cops, agents, and attorneys had no choice. It was just impossible to turn back, and the cat was out of the bag. I had blown the whistle, and all they could do now was dig a deeper hole.

On May 8, 2009 *Minneapolis Star Tribune* reporter David Chanen repeated some of the same allegations Lyden made in 2008 and a whole lot more. The headline was "Did Minneapolis police officer spin lies?" The article read, "Lt. Michael Keefe, whom the FBI now described as a threat, has been suspended over alleged rumors he spread about other officers and agents investigating corruption in a task force that he supervised." I considered it the equivalent of a shotgun blast to the head. With the help of seemingly corrupt law enforcement officers, Chanen and the *Star Tribune* ended my career. Lyden and his news station, KMSP FOX 9 News, wounded me badly, and Chanen and the *Star Tribune* put the final bullet in me. These were two news reporters who never seemed to have the courage or integrity to meet with me face-to-face and get my side of the story—the truth. I was labeled for life as an unhinged cop by criminals with badges who have been protected by the FBI. No cop on earth could ever recover from what I found to be such calculated defamation. A cop spinning lies? Game over. End of story. I could never quit and go work somewhere else. My career in law enforcement was over. Ironically, there were lots of cops, and quite possibly FBI agents as well, spinning lies, and only a federal grand jury and a special prosecutor can untangle their massive web of very intentional deceit.

Chanen also made reference to me giving a statement to Internal Affairs about the corruption, so who told him about that? Like Lyden's story, it was 100 percent fake news! In my mind, it was criminal. These were not law-enforcement officers blowing the whistle on corruption; these were law enforcement officers using the media to further their crimes. It was the media at its absolute worst. Chanen did quote my attorney, Fred Bruno, who said, "It doesn't surprise me that the suspension has happened now. The timing is somewhat curious." Bruno went further and said, "Keefe is a person of the highest moral integrity and his observations as an investigator have always been spot on." I appreciated the shout-out from Bruno, but it really didn't matter. It was literally impossible for me to fend off such a horrific attack by the largest newspaper in Minnesota. I believe that Chanen and Lyden should be called into court and compelled to reveal their sources. The practice of law enforcement officers using reporters to advance their crimes cannot be allowed to stand in America.

Within a few weeks, Minneapolis police union attorneys had me back on the job. Parker's unjust suspension claiming I had been "disruptive" had no standing, and there was nothing he could do.

On May 21, the FBI sent me a letter confirming they now had my case in Washington, DC, which is where it was supposed to have gone in the first place.

U.S. Department of Justice

Federal Bureau of Investigation

Washington, D. C. 20535-0001

May 21, 2009

Mr. Michael P. Keefe
▮▮▮▮▮▮▮▮▮▮

Dear Mr. Keefe:

    Your complaint was forwarded to the Initial Processing Unit (IPU), Internal Investigations Section (IIS), Inspection Division (INSD), Federal Bureau of Investigation (FBI), for review. The IIS/INSD is the FBI entity responsible for investigating allegations of serious misconduct or criminal activity on the part of FBI employees.

    You alleged that during the course of an FBI public corruption case involving officers of the Minneapolis Police Department, you discovered the informant, ▮▮▮ altered his story on multiple occasions and may have lied regarding the involvement of several officers in corrupt activities. You alleged that FBI Agents were aware of ▮ lack of credibility but "chose to look the other way." You also alleged that the FBI never took the proper steps to certify the veracity of ▮▮▮ statements and may have coached ▮▮▮ on several occasions in order to mask his false statements.

    The purpose of this letter is to inform you that the IPU/INSD has reviewed your allegations, and your concerns will receive appropriate attention.

                                    Sincerely,

                                      Unit Chief
                                    Initial Processing Unit
                                    Inspection Division

FBI letter to Keefe, May 21, 2009, complaint now with FBI Inspections

A few days later, on June 3, 2009, Internal Affairs sergeant Zabel confirmed I never said anyone was being indicted after my boss, Inspector Lucy Gerold, asked for my opinion at a Third Precinct staff meeting. Sgt. Zabel interviewed everyone who was at the meeting, and they all confirmed I never said officers were being indicted. Shaw seemed to have made it all up. In a normally functioning police department, Shaw would have immediately been suspended, relieved of duty, and terminated for falsely accusing me, but the MPD was not a normally functioning police department. Shaw was never disciplined for anything—not one thing. It was all swept under the rug.

Years later, through civil depositions, I would discover that on July 13, 2009, a high-ranking assistant US attorney for the state of Minnesota, Thomas Granger, sent a letter of appreciation to Deputy Chief Parker commending Officer Denton for his role in the public corruption case. It was interesting that it mentioned only Denton. Denton's cell phone and the MPD's public information officer log seemingly linked him to both media attacks on me. Was this a thank-you for the public attacks on me? My attorneys have no doubt it was. Ironically, Granger was copied on FBI agent Irving's letter to me in May 2009, seeking a meeting. So Granger certainly knew I contacted the inspector general's Chicago field office and blew the whistle on alleged corruption surrounding the Roberts case. Yet he took the time to draft a letter of appreciation to an officer involved in the same case that the Minneapolis FBI eventually sent to FBI Inspections in Washington DC for investigation. Needless to say, Granger's letter of appreciation to Denton warrants a great deal of scrutiny.

Did assistant US attorney Granger or the US attorney for Minnesota make the decision to cover up the exculpatory evidence (Jackson's apparent lies)? Somebody made that decision. If it wasn't Granger, Irving, or the Minneapolis FBI SAC, all eyes are on others, maybe even former FBI director Robert Mueller and former US attorney general Roberto Gonzales. Denton implied during his state deposition that the feds could have been behind the media attacks, and I believe FBI agent Turner was involved in the first media attack. Furthermore, two of Granger's subordinate attorneys, Stahl and Schultz, who went after me in 2007 and 2009, also signed the bizarre letter of appreciation to Denton just two months after the trial. Attorneys who have reviewed this case at length have no doubt it was an arrogant thank-you letter for the media attacks. Denton never testified, so why was he recognized by the attorneys?

None of it surprised me. Capt. Miller and I tried to have Denton removed from VOTF when I took over the task force in 2007, but Major Jim Owens found out about the pending transfer and stopped it. I warned Owens that Denton was a problem, but it didn't matter. This was the MPD, and ethics and integrity were optional.

The conclusion of Officer Roberts's trial and the passage of time did not alleviate any stress inside the MPD, Minneapolis FBI, or the Minneapolis US Attorney's office. They still had my inspector general complaint to deal with, which had now been advanced to FBI Inspections in Washington, DC. The summer of 2009 had Deputy Chief Parker and his friends on edge. They never knew from one day to the next whether FBI Inspections or deputy US Marshals were going to come knocking to investigate. The FBI never told the MPD what they were doing. They left the MPD in the dark, and all that did was cause the powers that be in the police department and city attorney's office to act even more irrational and unhinged.

In the fall of 2009, Parker started another seemingly phony public relations campaign. I knew right away Parker was up to no good. I had seen this dog-and-pony show a few months earlier, before Roberts's trial. In an August 2009 letter to the chief, mayor, city council, and rank and file, Parker said the MPD holds its 1,100 employees to the highest degree of professionalism. He went further and said, "I take investigations of complaints against our officers seriously." Parker kept up his campaign and sent out another citywide email. This time it was targeted to protect Shaw's seeming misconduct. He didn't mention Shaw by name, but the police union was all over him. Shaw's calling me into Internal Affairs in June 2008 made it clear to the police union that Shaw and others were out of control. In this latest propaganda email, Parker said, "I stand by my internal affairs staff. They may have have the most difficult job in law enforcement." Really? What a joke! What about street cops working overnight hours? Parker seemed desperate, and he had made himself look like a fool again. Parker went on to say, "They are hard working, honorable, and of high integrity." Parker was using email to protect himself and his friends. Unfortunately for him, attorneys I have consulted with informed me that it could be considered possible wire fraud.

The police union kept up the pressure on Parker, and in late September, Parker sent out another email, in which he told the rank and file, "The Federation [police union] claims that they have not attacked IAD investigators is very disingenuous. There is plenty of documentation to show otherwise. I also want to make it clear that the commander of IAD works for me and is following my directions." With that statement, Parker arrogantly, yet unwittingly, took ownership of perhaps all the corruption inside the MPD and Internal Affairs.

Parker seemed scared to death of me and the DOJ joining forces and coming after him. But he had an ace in his pocket: the two FBI agents who came forward and asked him to remove me and requested he not to tell me the real reason for my removal from VOTF. The real reason was because I refused to look the other way when I believed Jackson was lying about officers he claimed were corrupt. However, the card was not an ace. It would go only so far. So what was behind this latest public relations campaign?

Parker was getting ready to demote me, and what he was saying in those propaganda letters and emails was that his internal affairs unit was beyond reproach, but I knew that was not true. I was getting what I deserved, according to Parker. In reality, what he seemed to be telling the rank and file was, "If you cross me or speak out, I will bury you just like I have Lieutenant Keefe." The MPD had only about eight hundred officers; the rest were civilians. The rumor mill was always full, and I knew Parker was going after me for standing up to him and his cronies.

On September 28, 2009, Parker and the MPD took everything to another level and launched another attack. They knew I had turned them in to the Justice Department. They knew full well I had never spread any false rumors about cops being indicted, but nevertheless, somebody in the city attorney's office, likely in concert with Deputy Chief Parker and Major Wesley Yates, came up with the idea of demoting me to sergeant and giving me an order not to talk to anyone outside the MPD about my concerns of internal corruption. This was done under the guise of a performance improvement plan (PIP). In other words, they put what felt to me like a gag order on me not to talk to any outside agencies regarding my concerns of internal corruption. This definitely had to be the dumbest stunt yet. If it wasn't in writing, nobody would ever have believed it. It was right out of *Saturday Night Live*, a "Wayne's World" special, but it wasn't funny. It was sick and demented.

Years later I would find out that assistant city attorney Tilly Heck, Major Wesley Yates, and Captain Carter Reed were behind the language written in this document. Remember: Yates was sitting right next to Parker when he confessed the cover story was bogus in 2007, and now here he was in the fall of 2009 telling his lackey, Reed, according to his deposition, how to silence me for allegedly being disruptive. Yates was desperately trying to retire early so he could move back home to North Dakota and start a second career as a schoolteacher, and the last thing he wanted was for anyone in city hall or the media to get wind that he and the MPD were involved in a massive case of alleged corruption—especially one that was seemingly racially motivated.

So Yates told Reed to write up a so-called performance improvement plan, the PIP, since I was such a bad employee and causing so much "disruption." When Reed explained this during his deposition, my attorneys and I could not get over the level of stupidity. How stupid could these people be? Quite frankly, they could be very stupid. Needless to say, the real objective was to stop me from communicating with the Justice Department. It seemed to be another pretext—nothing more than a gag order to keep me from exposing corruption. This was another blunder, just like the silly cover story. And once again, Reed testified during his deposition that Yates was right in the middle of it. Reed told me and my attorneys that Yates told him how to write it. So there you had it, a high-ranking Minneapolis police commander was the architect behind a document written under the guise that it was a performance improvement plan, likely to keep me from exposing internal corruption. The ridiculous PIP was so disingenuous it wasn't even written on official MPD letterhead. It looked like something a kid would draft. Yates was deeply involved in the corruption, and he would seem to get more involved as time went on. In my mind, it was all nothing but retaliation for me turning them all in to the US Department of Justice.

The bogus PIP alleged that I was "disruptive," and I was now being demoted to sergeant for being disruptive. Sgt. Zabel had confirmed that I never spread any false rumors about other officers, and I was never disruptive, but it didn't matter, because Parker and Yates didn't seem to be following any rules or regulations. Even if an officer was disruptive, it wasn't grounds for a demotion. Demotions are for poor performance. Demoting me likely violated policy and state employment law, but again, it didn't matter. They were determined to humiliate and destroy me, whatever the cost. They demoted me for something I never did, but they didn't care; they were above the law. In fact, they *were* the law. The demotion cost me thousands of dollars in lost pay, overtime, and pension benefits. It was another knife in the back.

In October 2009, my attorneys sued the MPD. After five state depositions and thirty federal depositions over the course of five years, the truth slowly came out—but not before the MPD launched a few more assaults.

Performance Improvement Plan
Sergeant Michael Keefe

Sergeant Michael Keefe will:

- Convey through the chain of command any policy or other concerns.

- Attend bi-weekly meetings with ▉▉▉▉▉▉▉▉▉▉▉▉▉▉▉▉▉▉▉▉
  The purpose of these meetings will be to track your progress with the Performance Improvement Plan (PIP) and to provide you with feedback on any issues or improvements identified. These meetings will be held in City Hall, room 100 for your privacy.

- Understand and appreciate different perspectives that co-workers may have. Display professionalism when speaking to co-workers and all citizens, expressing your opinions to them based upon fact and not opinion or conjecture.

  Follow all MPD polices and procedures.

This agreement will be in place for a minimum of one year from the date of the agreement at which time it will be reviewed for any necessary changes. If you need clarification on any of the expectations set out in this plan, please contact ▉▉▉▉▉▉▉▉▉▉.

Failure to follow these objectives may result in discipline.

I have read and received a copy of this Performance Improvement Plan.

_____
Sergeant Michael Keefe

Sept 28, 2009
Date

(PIP) dated 9/28/2009

CHAPTER 7
SERGEANT BURT

MAJ. YATES AND CAPT. REED PUT WHAT I FELT WAS A GAG ORDER ON me in the fall of 2009, ordering me not to go outside of the department with my concerns of internal corruption. The first order of the PIP was "Convey through the chain of command any policy or **other concerns**." In other words, "You cannot talk to anyone outside of the MPD unless you go through us first." So according to the PIP, the seemingly delusional city of Minneapolis owned me, as if I were a piece of property. I had no rights. So if I had "other concerns"—about something like the weather, for example—apparently I was supposed to run them by my superiors in the MPD. Their audacity was surreal, not to mention that the order was, I believe, absolutely illegal. Another bullet point said, "Express your opinions based upon facts and not opinion or conjecture." What? I was not allowed to express my opinion? The definition of an opinion, according to most dictionaries, is "A view or judgment formed about something, not necessarily based on fact or knowledge."

I wasn't about to keep quiet. I was committed to exposing the wrongdoing, so the first thing I did was quietly seek out a retired cop who was working as a private detective. A friend of a friend told me about a retired Bloomington, Minnesota, cop who was also a former Minnesota Bureau of Criminal Apprehension agent. Perfect. A real cop with investigative experience. A guy who would immediately get it. And get it he did. It was an absolute blessing.

Jim Hessell[was an experienced man who carried himself well. He was modest and unassuming, but probably more importantly, he was absolutely competent and beyond reproach. His first order of business was to do what an honest and ethical internal affairs investigator should have done: interview the Faribault police chief, his captain, and the Rice County Sheriff, and find out what I told them. Question number one: Did I give them a short briefing, as Assistant US Attorney Folk told me, or did I illegally give them extensive confidential information without authorization, as VOTF officers seem to have claimed? Hessell took statements from all three of them, and they all confirmed that all I had done was give them a very basic heads-up, just as I said, and just as Folk had asked me to do. In no uncertain terms, Hessell confirmed that the infamous cover story that I violated a federal wiretap and made an unauthorized disclosure was an absolute lie! End of story. Hessell provided me and my attorneys with typed statements from the chief, his captain, and the sheriff.

When VOTF officers made up that ridiculous story, the first thing Shaw should have done was call all of them in for taped statements. If Shaw had done so and interviewed the Faribault chief, his captain, and the Rice County sheriff, she could have quickly exonerated me. Her next step would have been to file paperwork to fire all the VOTF officers behind the cover story, but she didn't do that, because I believe she was working with them to attack me.

In 2010 my attorneys deposed Officer Denton in state court. My attorney in state court was Marshall H. Tanick, a brilliant attorney and a well-known Twin-Cities First Amendment attorney who was highly respected. Tanick was a go-to-guy for First Amendment issues and a whole lot more. He was nobody to mess with in a courtroom and certainly not during a deposition. In the beginning of his deposition, Denton made it clear that he didn't believe the attorneys had his cell phone records. In fact, he said it was his understanding that no such records were available. Denton was so bold and arrogant that he emphatically told Attorney Tanick, "I'm telling you I've never supplied any information about Mike Keefe to anybody in the media." Tanick pressed him further and asked, "At any time?" Denton replied in the affirmative: "At any time." Moments later in the deposition, and for the first time, Tanick showed Denton some of his cell phone records showing he called *Star Tribune* reporter David Chanen's number. Denton turned snow white, but he still insisted he never gave Chanen or anyone in the media defamatory information about me. Then Tanick showed Denton all the records. At that point, Denton had to have known his testimony did not conform to the truth, so he changed his story and now he said he "did not recall" giving Chanen false and defamatory information. Denton continued to waver back and forth from being adamant he had not provided any information to "I don't recall" or "I don't remember."

Tanick also asked Denton whether he ever discussed the May 2009 *Star Tribune* story about me (the second media attack) with anyone. Denton denied it but later claimed he remembered talking about the article with Capt. Wright and Officer Evans on the day the article was written. As the deposition went on, Denton seemed to become more erratic. Tanick set Denton up again by allowing Denton to confirm his friendly relationship with Chanen and KMSP-TV reporter Tom Lyden. Denton arrogantly proclaimed, "I've had multiple contacts with the media." Denton went even further and said, "I have called Chanen just to say how's it going." Denton continued and said he had called Chanen just to let him know when he liked a story he had written. All of this was from a low-level officer who was precluded by policy from talking to the media about police department policy in the first place.

Denton's bravado was endless, as he claimed to have "sources in the *Star Tribune* and some news channels." Denton was on a roll. Then he said, "Tom Lyden is a good source. David Chanen is a good source." Denton boasted he told Internal Affairs that he talked to Lyden and Chanen frequently and that the reporters allegedly supplied him with information as well. Denton was so full of himself he even admitted he had let the reporters into the VOTF office. Tanick, with the help of Denton himself and his overinflated ego, confirmed a cozy relationship. Once Tanick sealed the relationship between Denton and the reporters, he pressed Denton on why his cell phone records linked him to Chanen on the eve of the Roberts trial in May of 2009. Denton went into serious panic mode and proceeded to say the dumbest thing imaginable. He told Tanick he didn't even know whether Chanen was on the other end of the line while they were talking!

And just like that, Denton seemingly confessed to being Chanen's source for the second media attack and didn't even realize it. He admitted to talking to somebody at the *Star Tribune* on the eve of the second media attack, but he had no idea whom he was talking to.

Denton's face said it all. I thought he was caught, and that he knew it; he looked like a deer in the headlights. Everyone in the room was in shock. The steno raised her eyebrows. Tanick sarcastically asked Denton whether he had been talking to the janitor. I wanted to laugh. Tanick had just leveled Denton big time. Denton had seemingly confessed to calling somebody at the *Star Tribune* on the eve of the second media attack. He looked like a complete moron. He was on an island by himself, but true to form, he shot back at Tanick and told him that he didn't have any idea who was on the other end of the line and that it wasn't his job to help him figure it out! Denton seemed to become more bizarre and erratic, and at one point he claimed that perhaps I was Chanen's source for the negative story about myself. My attorneys and I began to wonder whether he was under the influence of drugs. A few minutes later, Denton tried to blame Deputy Chief Parker for leaking information to Chanen. Denton was acting like a caged wild animal. Tanick quickly pointed out that the May 2009 story (the second media attack) noted that Parker and I allegedly could not be reached for comment. Denton then speculated that Chanen was lying to cover for Parker. I thought Denton was cornered, and he had nowhere to go.

Was Denton on the verge of giving up Deputy Chief Parker? Denton didn't stop with his accusations. He went further and now alleged that the responsible party might be the FBI. It was an absolute bombshell. We just had a sworn Minneapolis police officer under oath allege the FBI might be the source of the second media attack—the most horrific media attack of the two. Denton continued and gave us examples of why it might be the FBI. So the bigger question is, Was the FBI the source, or one of the sources, of the second media attack? At this point, Denton was in deep, and every word out of his mouth seemed to me to be a misstep. He should have just shut up, but his arrogance and insecurity seemed to take over. Was the FBI a source, or was Denton just desperately running for cover and burning every bridge along the way? Regardless, Denton implied that the FBI was involved in the second media attack, which would put them squarely in the middle of a potential RICO case. If the FBI wasn't involved, they needed to step up and help me identify the source and clear their name from this horrific attack, but to date all the FBI has done is hide.

After I was removed from my command, my sergeants, Haverly and Eklund, put in for transfers and moved on to other units. Capt. Miller retired and moved to Florida. The command staff put Captain Heidi Kirby in charge of the criminal investigations division, and Lieutenant Lance Johnston and Sergeant Charlie Whitehorse were in charge of VOTF, along with a rookie, Sergeant Chue Moua. Moua was a very smart man and a top-notch cop. He was put in charge of an undercover drug-smuggling operation with the DEA involving opium coming into the country from Southeast Asia, so he was out of the picture. Whitehorse was near retirement, and he just didn't seem to care anymore. He had serious health problems and needed medical coverage; otherwise, he would have retired a long time ago. He was there physically, but mentally he was suffering. He was a nice man, and I thought the bad VOTF cops ran over him like a freight train. Johnston was also a very likeable man and the son of a prominent local attorney, but he had zero interest in being a cop, let alone a supervisor. He was going to law school at night, and his job was just a formality. It seemed to me that he let the VOTF cops run wild, and run wild they did. When it came time to sign paperwork and run the unit, I thought he was like Lieutenant Colonel Henry Blake from the 1970s sitcom *M*A*S*H*, who always signed whatever Radar put in front of him. Neither Whitehorse or Johnston were ever involved in anything nefarious; I just didn't think they were involved in anything, period. It was the stereotypical lackadaisical leadership one can find only in government work.

Captain Heidi Kirby was an attractive woman with a thirst for money and the high life. She lived in an expensive condo in downtown Minneapolis, and she knew how to use her good looks and charm to get her way. She spent most of her time in fancy coffee shops, restaurants, and stores in downtown Minneapolis and the suburbs. Like Johnston, she seemed to have no interest in police work. Her only concern was money. Kirby was given Capt. Miller's job the moment he retired thanks to her friends in high places. Once Kirby secured her new assignment, she hand-picked Whitehorse and Johnston because, I believe, she knew they would not question anything she did. She had no say in picking Moua, but it didn't matter, because he had a different assignment outside of the task force. He spent all his time with the narcotics unit and the DEA. She was free to run the table.

Sgt. Burt and others recognized the lack of leadership in VOTF, so Burt stepped up and put pen to paper and demanded accountability.

In March of 2010, unbeknownst to me, Sgt. Burt, a highly respected veteran Minneapolis police sergeant, walked into Minneapolis Police Internal Affairs and corroborated everything I had been saying about VOTF. It was an absolute nightmare for the police department and the City of Minneapolis. Any decent, self-respecting police department would have immediately said uncle and brought in an outside agency to investigate, but not the MPD. MPD commanders were not about to let any other agency investigate them or their friends.

Burt took the time to meticulously draft two sets of documents detailing alleged corruption inside of VOTF. The first set of documents was seven typed pages. Sgt. Burt held nothing back and detailed how VOTF officers were motivated by money and padding their pensions. Moreover, Burt noted that VOTF was seizing money from criminals and putting the money into a designated fund to be used for their overtime. In other words, the more money seized, the more overtime. Sergeant Burt noted how other law enforcement agencies were skeptical of the MPD and how MPD officers were allowed to "scam the system." The memo also noted that several officers witnessed wrongdoing but were afraid to come forward because VOTF officers were seemingly protected by the police administration. Burt said it was widely known that some VOTF officers were allegedly "untouchable" because of their relationship with Deputy Chief Parker and other commanders. Burt said he was told by Captain Heidi Kirby to focus on wiretaps and obtaining large cash seizures, and he noted how in 2009 some VOTF officers were almost doubling their salaries with overtime. Sgt. Burt outlined how VOTF officers were allegedly manipulating "surveillance details" and "investigations" for lucrative overtime on the weekend and evenings. He provided details and examples of how $12,000 was removed from a US Immigration and Customs Enforcement agent's account without the case agent's authorization, how $50,000 was abruptly pulled out of a Chicago drug deal and placed into the VOTF overtime account, and how a VOTF officer unsuccessfully tried to get Burt to illegally divert seizure funds into the VOTF account.

Sgt. Burt provided Internal Affairs with a second set of documents shortly after he came forward the first time. His second set of documents was more than five typed pages of detailed notes and one page of handwritten notes.

In his second set of documents, Burt once again noted how some VOTF officers were allegedly padding their paychecks with absurd amounts of overtime. He also noted how other law enforcement agencies refused to work with VOTF. I felt that Chief Dolan and Deputy Chief Parker persecuted me for holding other agencies accountable, but now they were seemingly allowing VOTF to run wild and destroy agency relationships. Burt detailed how the number-one objective of VOTF was making overtime, not taking down violent gangs and criminals. It was all about overtime and wiretaps to make more overtime. Sgt. Burt provided the names of officers, agents, and attorneys who could corroborate his complaint, but it didn't matter, because the department refused to investigate Burt's complaint. One of those federal agents who would corroborate the complaint was FBI agent Michelle O'Shea. She was hardworking and disciplined—everything you would expect from an FBI agent—and backing her up was assistant US attorney Nancy Hanson, an equally hardworking and respected government attorney just doing her job. They backed up Burt and Burt backed me up. It was a solid line of corroboration.

Sgt. Burt's complaints about corruption inside of VOTF were allegedly ignored and quietly shelved because the MPD did not want me or my attorneys to find out about Burt's complaint or, worse yet, get our hands on Burt's written documents detailing internal corruption. But by pure chance, Burt and I ran into each other in the MPD's Property and Evidence Unit about a year and half later. Burt told me about his Internal Affairs complaint, and I immediately called my attorneys, and they sent Burt a subpoena for a deposition.

Sgt. Burt was a highly respected undercover narcotics cop assigned to the US Drug Enforcement Administration task force when he walked into Internal Affairs and blew the whistle on corruption inside the VOTF unit. There should have been a full-scale criminal investigation. Burt provided Internal Affairs with several pages of detailed notes outlining allegations of theft of government funds, abuse of power under the color of law, racism, and a whole slew of corrupt tricks and deceit. The complaint mirrored what I had been saying for years, but it was shelved within a few days according to the deposition testimony of Captain Amelia Huffman. The officers Burt identified were seemingly above the law and had impunity to do whatever they wanted.

Burt provided details of how some VOTF officers were allegedly using seized money they funneled back into an exclusive overtime account for themselves and their friends. They allegedly set up the overtime account to become self-sufficient—no more dependency on the city or federal government for money. The more money and property they seized, the more they had in their account for overtime, meaning there was no need to beg the city and feds for money.

Sgt. Burt provided details about how $50,000 was allegedly seized from a drug deal in Chicago. Instead of letting the money flow through to get the drug dealers, they allegedly seized the money and put it into the VOTF overtime account. The DEA was livid when this happened, and that was the end of VOTF ties with the DEA. But again, there was no investigation, discipline, or accountability. The MPD may have thought when they attacked me that fellow officers would get the memo to keep quiet, but Sgt. Burt was an honest man with principles and integrity. He refused to stay quiet or back down to seemingly unethical cops and commanders in power.

So now, in early 2010, there was Burt's complaint and my lawsuit alleging corruption. At this point any normally functioning police department would have hit the brakes and brought in everyone to figure out what was going on if there truly was confusion. But in this case, nobody in the city attorney's office or the police administration seemed confused. So what did they do? They made the preposterous claim that Burt, despite all his evidence and the witnesses he offered, had a grudge to settle with Capt. Kirby, and just like that, Burt's complaint was squashed.

Deputy Chief Parker and his buddies must have been breathing a huge sigh of relief after Sgt. Burt's detailed Internal Affairs complaint was squashed, but that would be short-lived, because I was still coming after them with my civil attorneys and slowly building a criminal case. I was a veteran investigator, and I was confident my civil suit would expose corruption. I also knew that Capt. Reed and Maj. Yates's ridiculous PIP gave me a great opportunity to counterattack, and counterattack I did. On April 19, 2010, a month after Sgt. Burt made his first Internal Affairs complaint, I used an old FBI trick to humiliate the powers that be in the City of Minneapolis and the Minneapolis Police Department and simultaneously left a huge footprint for a future criminal investigation. It was a bold and stunning counterpunch. The police union told me not to do it, because they were afraid Parker would dupe the chief into firing me, but I did it anyway. I sent Deputy Chief Parker a letter requesting an Internal Affairs investigation of himself and his friends and all the misconduct. It was an old-fashioned FBI-style integrity test to see what a cop would do. And just like Burt's Internal Affairs complaint, they covered up my request, which was my third Internal Affairs complaint, with a lot of smoke and mirrors along the way.

I suspected Deputy Chief Parker would refuse to investigate Yates and Reed's PIP as well as himself and his allies and all their alleged misconduct, but it didn't matter, because I was building a paper trail for future depositions and criminal investigations. It didn't matter what

Parker or the city did; either way, they lost. They backed themselves into a corner with the PIP, the city hall attack, the media attacks, the cover story, and everything else, and I shoved it down their throat. I went further and gave Deputy Chief Parker a May 1 deadline to respond to my request. I knew Deputy Chief Parker would not respond, so I totally bypassed Parker, and on April 29 I sent Minneapolis police Chief Timothy Dolan and Internal Affairs director Captain Jerry Hess a detailed letter exposing how Wright, and Denton's cell phone records appeared to be linked to the first and second media attacks. I did not tell Dolan or Hess about Parker's calls to Chanen in the days preceding the second media attack, because I suspected that someone would tip Parker off; and sure enough, years later, my attorneys and I confirmed somebody tipped off Parker about those calls just before media attack number two. Parker's city cell phone was not directly linked to the second media attack on May 8, 2009. But three days before that media attack, on May 5, Parker talked to Chanen for ten minutes, and prior to that he and Chanen called each other back and forth on April 23 and April 28. My attorneys and I think it's unlikely the *Star Tribune* would have ever written what I found to be a seriously defamatory story about me on May 8 unless Chief Dolan, Deputy Chief Parker, FBI SSA Irving, the Minneapolis FBI SAC, Ralph Boelter, or someone higher up was one of the sources besides Wright and Denton. Chanen's sources have never been completely exposed to date, but a criminal probe would quickly solve that mystery.

I was demanding an investigation of the phone calls to the reporters, and everything else, but the police administration and Internal Affairs denied it. But I, unlike Sgt. Burt, had a pending civil suit, and it was too risky to bury everything as quickly as they seem to have done with Burt's complaint. They would have to try to make it look like a legitimate investigation, but all they did was make things worse for themselves.

Years later, we would discover that Internal Affairs Captain Hess was given marching orders to bury Burt's case within a few days and claim it was a personal thing between Burt and Capt. Kirby, and to seemingly stall my case as long as she could.

Hess was allegedly seeking legal advice from assistant city attorney Ernest Lyon on how to handle my complaint. Why in the world would a police commander need an attorney's advice on how to investigate a simple complaint? I believe he didn't, and some in the police union had nothing good to say about Lyon. He was considered by some to be unethical and deceptive. Regardless, I had them backed into a corner. No matter what they did, they lost. I had evidence of possible criminal misconduct on the part of high-ranking police commanders and several others. The cell phone evidence was overwhelming. They contacted the media to further their alleged crimes. It warranted a big-time outside investigation. Lyon and Hess decided they would play dumb, roll the dice, and go with the old "attorney-client privilege" game and allegedly shared my cell phone evidence and everything else with the prime suspect, Deputy Chief Parker. It seems they literally tipped him off under the guise of attorney-client privilege and let him decide what to do. My attorneys and I were in absolute shock!

They called up one of the suspects, Deputy Chief Parker, and allegedly provided him with an attorney and the evidence, and just as expected, he shut everything down. But first he gave Hess an order to look into my third Internal Affairs complaint.

My first complaint was against VOTF officers after I was removed from my command, my second complaint was against Shaw, and now this complaint was about the media attacks, the restrictive PIP, and basically everything else. Hess would later admit in his deposition testimony that everything he did was controlled by supervisors from start to finish. Hess seemingly whitewashed everything. He may have thought he was clever, but all he really did was likely put himself in the middle of a future criminal investigation. He should have issued subpoenas for all three officers' city cell phones and landline phones; searched their work spaces, their city computers, and their city vehicles; contacted the Minnesota BCA or the St. Paul Police Department and requested a parallel criminal investigation; and called in Denton and given him a compelled Garrity warning and demanded the truth, but he did none of the above.

Remember: Hess claimed Burt's complaint was a personal vendetta. Burt seemingly gave Hess and the MPD a ton of evidence. His reputation was stellar, and he was well respected. Nevertheless, Hess or one of his cohorts hatched the ridiculous vendetta story. Vendetta over what? Who came up with that cover story?

Anyway, now it was time for Hess to deal with my third Internal Affairs complaint about Wright, Denton, Parker, and their apparent links to the reporters. Hess played dumb on everything I pointed out in my complaint. For example, I advised Hess about Denton's links to reporter Tom Lyden via the public information officer's log. Hess claimed that Kare 11 TV reporter Trish Volpe and WCCO-TV reporter Jason DeRusha might be the sources.

The main problem with that was that neither of them had done a story about me. Moreover, the author of the log, Sergeant Jesse Garcia, wrote, "Joe Denton- Channel 9, letter from city atty." All of these facts were written on Garcia's January 24, 2008, log and related to my case. Fox 9 News is Lyden's employer. Furthermore, Denton was forced to admit he had talked to Lyden in the past, and no other media outlets reported anything. Nothing was on the log about Volpe, DeRusha, or their respective news stations. Hess glossed over everything I pointed out in my very detailed third Internal Affairs complaint in 2010.

I felt this egregious conduct required compelled statements using the power of the landmark *Garrity* decision, which would have ordered Denton, Wright, and Parker to talk. The first order of business would have been to bring in the lowest-ranking officer, Denton, and force him to give up everyone or face immediate termination. An outside agency would have done just that and eventually requested testimony from Wright and Parker. Denton might have been given leniency to give up his superiors, but regardless, Hess seemingly covered their tracks.

To make matters worse, the MPD did not have a conflict-of-interest policy that would mandate the chief of police to farm out complaints against him or other commanders. In other words, the MPD did not have an ounce of transparency or accountability. Burt and I had evidence of alleged criminal misconduct on the part of several high-ranking commanders and officers that should have resulted in their termination and criminal charges, but it was not investigated.

Capt. Hess's seeming games were nothing but smoke and mirrors. All the effort he put forth playing dumb only made him seem to me all the more culpable. The 1967 landmark case of *Garrity v. New Jersey* gave every police department in the United States the right to order officers into internal affairs and make them give truthful statements or face immediate termination. That is all Capt. Hess had to do. It was that simple. All he had to do was call in Denton, and just like that I believe it would have been game over. *Garrity* has been preached at police academies around the country for years, and Hess should have known better.

Officer Denton would likely have thrown everyone under the bus in a matter of minutes, as he almost did during his state court deposition. The cell phone evidence and public information officer's log linking him to the media attacks on me were irrefutable and overwhelming. If the Garrity warning had been used, it would have been the beginning of the end for the cops, agents, and attorneys. No lawyer in the country could have refuted the phone calls or saved any of them.

The apparent criminal misconduct of the MPD and the City of Minneapolis was moving full steam ahead in November of 2010 when Major Anna Wagner, Parker's number-one enforcer, sent me a letter threatening me with termination if I made any more "false allegations" about corruption in the MPD. This would literally be impossible to believe if she had not put it in writing, but she had, and during her deposition, Wagner claimed a Minneapolis city attorney helped her write the letter. Moreover, Maj. Wagner sent me that letter after Sgt. Burt had filed his detailed Internal Affairs complaints that corroborated everything I had been saying since 2007. Think about it; a high-ranking Minneapolis Police commander threatened to fire me for making false allegations, likely knowing full well, I believe, that everything I had said was virtually 100 percent corroborated by Sgt. Burt. The MPD was clearly out of control and operating way outside the boundaries of established government protocol.

Minneapolis
City of Lakes

Police Department

Timothy J. Dolan
Chief of Police

350 South 5th Street – Room 130
Minneapolis MN 55415-1389

Office 612 673-2736
TTY 612 673-2157

November 16, 2010

Sergeant Michael Keefe
Minneapolis Police Department
First Precinct Investigations
19 North 4th Street
Minneapolis, MN 55401

Sergeant Keefe,

Pursuant to your written allegations of *"Police Misconduct"* provided to Internal Affairs on 4/29/10 an investigation has been completed by Internal Affairs. As a result of this investigation, no misconduct has been uncovered as alleged and the matter is closed.

While the MPD encourages employees who believe that others may be involved in criminal or other types of misconduct to come forward, in this case, your allegations have not been supported by evidence. In this case, you again made very specific statements that MPD employees were involved in criminal and unethical activity as well as that they have a history of making racial remarks. These were represented by you as fact rather than opinion.

As you recall, you have previously been disciplined for making similar allegations without merit before. Further, in 2009 you underwent a fitness for duty exam which determined that your ability to perform your duties as a Minneapolis Police Officer was contingent on your letting go of your belief that other MPD employees are under investigation, indictment or involved in criminal activity.

This letter should serve as notice that further allegations of this nature absent facts or evidence to support them, may result in discipline up to and including termination from employment with the City of Minneapolis.

Sincerely,

Minneapolis Police Department

311
City Information
and Services

www.ci.minneapolis.mn.us
Affirmative Action Employer

(WAGNER THREAT) 11/16/2010

In fall of 2010, the MPD was backed into a corner and there was nowhere to turn. My lawyers were setting up depositions, and the only way out for the targeted officers would be relentless false testimony. They had nowhere to turn because the FBI had more than its own share of potential criminal culpability. It was a case like no other in the history of the United States. The FBI, the premier law enforcement agency in the United States, could not help any cop who may have wanted to back up Sgt. Burt or me, because the FBI had blood on their hands, just like the MPD.

The MPD and the FBI had created a massive case of corruption.

CHAPTER 8
CITY HALL AMBUSH

IN THE FALL OF 2010, OFFICER GRADY LOFTUS WAS THE VERY FIRST officer deposed under federal court jurisdiction. I knew Officer Loftus was a good man, and within minutes of his deposition it became clear to me and my attorneys we were uncovering a massive case of alleged corruption. In no uncertain terms, it was clear that we likely had a federal Title 18 Conspiracy to Obstruct Justice case, civil rights violations, and a lot more—perhaps a RICO case. Loftus had nothing to hide, and he put it all on the table, as a good cop should. It was mind-boggling. He stated that Deputy Chief Parker sent out an email on Friday, May 8, 2009, at 9:38 a.m. with a copy of my Minnesota driver's license photo to Mayor Rybak, his deputy mayor, and others, claiming I was mentally unstable and that the recipients were to proceed with caution. In that very sentence, Loftus provided the framework for a massive case of alleged criminal misconduct. Deputy Chief Parker was allegedly spreading a horrific lie on the Friday before the start of Officer Roberts's trial.

Loftus was bewildered because I had a good reputation. Loftus said Maj. Wagner told him I could enter city hall as usual. So why was there an alert? It didn't make any sense. Wagner told him the MPD was advised of a "threat" from the FBI. None of it seemed to make any sense, but my attorneys and I knew exactly what Officer Loftus was talking about. Remember: two days before Deputy Chief Parker suspended me on the eve of Roberts's trial, FBI agent Peterson put out a third office alert on me after I refused to meet with FBI SSA Irving. The alert said,

"This is a personnel safety matter. PROCEED WITH CAUTION." It seemed to be retaliation because I had refused to talk to the FBI. What did they want, anyway? Did they want to help settle my civil suit? Were they planning on framing me if I talked to them? Were they going to try to pay me off? The FBI knew they could never intimidate or scare me. But what was the real reason behind the bogus alert? Only agent Peterson can answer that question. She might if she is given immunity.

At any rate, like Parker's attack on the eve of the trial, it was seemingly designed to destroy my credibility in case I testified. America's premier law enforcement agency had just bottomed out. I believe it could be seen as witness tampering and obstruction of justice, just to name a few of the potential crimes. If I was a threat to anyone, as the FBI and Parker claimed, why wasn't my badge and his ID confiscated, per policy? Moreover, if I was a threat to anyone, then why was I allowed into city hall? Nothing made sense.

Loftus said Parker sent him an email twelve minutes later, at 9:50 a.m., and told him to advise building security and the city council that I was a threat. What had I done? Loftus said the building supervisor, Steve Parsons, told him that he talked to Maj. Wagner and that Wagner told him it wasn't that serious.

But then why the alert and further potential destruction of my reputation and career? What was going on? The sheriff's office wasn't placed on alert, and they were in city hall. Remember: Sheriff Stanek, attorney Fred Bruno, and I had an agreement to keep everything quiet. Moreover, when this happened, Parker and the FBI may very well have known Stanek was essentially supporting me by keeping quiet. It's quite possible the loose lips of the inspector general's office told Parker and the FBI that Stanek was quietly supporting me and Bruno by keeping quiet. Hence, the Sheriff's office was not advised of the city hall attack. Perhaps Parker feared Stanek would cause a rift if he heard about the alert, knowing it was unfounded and, to me, nothing but apparent retaliation. Loftus said he told the mayor's staff that I had never been a problem and he did not see me as a threat. Nevertheless, neither Chief Dolan nor Deputy Chief Parker ever rescinded the alert. Officer Loftus said the alert would have prevented me from meeting with the mayor. Were they afraid I was going to personally tell the mayor about all the corruption? Only a full-scale criminal investigation can answer that question.

Depositions and drama continued throughout 2011. My attorneys were demanding a multimillion-dollar settlement, and the police administration could not honestly explain to the mayor and city council why the attorneys wanted so much money. They had no choice but to refuse to settle. I believe they were hoping all the stress would cause me to have a relapse of cancer. No matter how you cut it, it felt sick and cruel that law enforcement officers could act with so much malice. An admission on Deputy Chief Parker's part that he and his friends unjustly went after black police officers by covering up exculpatory evidence just wasn't an option. They had to roll the dice.

One of the first moves the city attorneys made in 2011 was to get a court order demanding all my medical records and tax income statements. They were looking to see whether I was beating cancer or diagnosed as mentally ill, but once again they struck out. I was healthy, and my finances were spot on. All along, they knew I was nothing but an honest cop who refused to frame anyone.

In early 2011, Capt. Hess, the Internal Affairs director, was deposed for the first time. During his deposition, he admitted he was aware the Hennepin County Sheriff's office and the Minnesota Bureau of Criminal Apprehension could conduct criminal investigations of police misconduct, and he reluctantly agreed that a case against a senior officer to whom one reports could constitute a conflict of interest. No kidding. Hess seemed to be initially stonewalling, and he was forced to admit he never interviewed Deputy Chief Parker about making calls to reporter David Chanen.

Hess also admitted that Maj. Wagner's November 16, 2010, letter threatening me with termination was not policy. A major should never get involved in a complaint. The job of a major is to sit back and let your subordinates bring you a case when it's finished. Hess claimed he did not recall whether Wagner ever saw my 2010 Internal Affairs complaint, which was convenient, because if she had, that meant Hess likely tipped her off and Wagner was one of the suspects. Capt. Hess said Maj. Wagner and Deputy Chief Parker told him how to handle my 2010 internal affairs complaint from beginning to end. **Hence, they were going to be the judge, jury, and executioner of the Internal Affairs complaint against them.** It was surreal. Attorney Ward shook his head, and I have no doubt it rattled Hess. Ward held his cards close to his vest, but this was so outrageous and preposterous he let him know it, and it clearly scared him. He must have known it was wrong, and he seemed to waste no time throwing Parker and Wagner under the bus. He couldn't spill the beans fast enough, and then he dropped a bomb on the entire city.

Capt. Hess said he had a meeting with Deputy Chief Parker, Maj. Wagner, and assistant city attorney Ernest Lyon, and they all discussed my third Internal Affairs complaint in 2010! Unbelievable! When he said this, he literally blew the lid off his deposition. In a split second, Albert Goins raised his voice and immediately stopped the deposition and called the presiding US magistrate, Judge Steven Rau. Assistant city attorney Tim Boone was representing Hess, and he never saw this coming, and I could clearly see he was in shock.

The Minneapolis police Internal Affairs director had just admitted to sitting down with two of the suspects identified in my written Internal Affairs complaint and discussed how to proceed. What the hell was going on? Since when does a police Internal Affairs director sit down with any police officer and a city attorney and decide what they are going to do with a complaint they have for excessive force, profanity, or any other possible violation? It would never happen. It would be the same as sitting down with a burglary suspect, providing him an attorney, and asking the burglar how to proceed. My attorneys were livid, and they weren't afraid to show it. In my opinion, it was irrefutable collusion.

The judge immediately ordered an in-camera review, and within days Capt. Hess was in his chambers. (An in-camera review is when a judge stops a proceeding and privately looks at confidential or sensitive evidence to determine what, if any, evidence may be used, and then issues a confidential, sealed nonpublic ruling.)

We may never know what Hess told the judge, but he was undoubtedly well versed by city attorneys in what *not* to say to the judge by the time he got into his chambers. Apparently they all felt as though it was okay to provide legal representation to two officers who were being accused of potential criminal misconduct by another officer, and assistant city attorney Lyon seemingly did it under the guise of attorney-client privilege. After that bit of drama, all the depositions were put on hold until Judge Rau interviewed Capt. Hess in his chambers and made his ruling.

Unfortunately, Judge Rau wasn't aware of the big picture, and the public may never know what Hess told him without a full-scale criminal investigation. But I believe Hess may have lied to save himself and Lyon, because if Hess had spilled all the beans, my attorneys and I believe, Judge Rau would have sanctioned the city. I suspect Hess never told Rau the whole story. It's also highly unlikely Hess told Judge Rau about Sgt. Burt's complaint, which was relevant and part of the big picture.

After Hess was interviewed by Judge Rau, the depositions were restarted.

Internal Affairs investigator Sergeant Gemma Shaw was deposed in January of 2011 for the first time. During this deposition and two follow-up depositions, we discovered that Shaw repeatedly seemed to have violated MPD policy and met with officers she wanted to take statements from outside of the Minneapolis Police Internal Affairs office, with no tape recordings of those conversations. Nevertheless, Shaw admitted Officer Hardy relayed the cover story about me allegedly violating the wiretap rules (unauthorized disclosure) during the Tre-Tre Crips case in Faribault, to Internal Affairs, Capt. Robinson, and perhaps others, but Shaw never drafted any paperwork to have Hardy suspended, fired, or charged criminally for making the seemingly false police report.

Sgt. Shaw reluctantly admitted that Minneapolis police officers are routinely fired for lying to Internal Affairs, but she did nothing to Officer Hardy when he allegedly lied about the bogus cover story. Furthermore, the FBI, according to Shaw, made it clear to her that I never violated the wiretap rules when I briefed the Faribault chief, his captain, and the Rice County sheriff. In other words, the cover story that I violated the wiretap rules and made an unauthorized disclosure was totally unfounded. Yet Hardy and others in VOTF allegedly told Shaw and Capt. Robinson it was true.

Shaw confirmed that Hardy claimed in his Internal Affairs complaint that I violated the wiretap rules and made an unauthorized disclosure. However, Shaw said the FBI told her, "Lt. Keefe was not going to be accused of that misconduct." In other words, once again, I never made an unauthorized disclosure when I briefed the Faribault police chief, his captain, and the Rice County sheriff. So I never did anything wrong. I never violated the wiretap rules. Period. Furthermore, it affirmed that the infamous cover story that claimed I did was completely unfounded. When she was asked why she didn't follow up with criminal charges and discipline for Officer Hardy, she stared at the ceiling for what seemed like an hour and finally said, "**I don't have an answer.**" Sgt. Shaw also admitted she never taped Hardy before his "official" interview, which I believe was required per department policy. The assistant city attorney sitting next to Shaw, David Nelson, should have immediately notified the city attorney, the chief of police, and the mayor of Shaw's seeming criminal misconduct, but apparently he did not, or if he did, then the acting city attorney, the chief, and the mayor did not pursue it. Once again, it's another unanswered question. The civil case should have ended immediately. Nelson seems to have had knowledge that the Internal Affairs investigator had seemingly committed several crimes, and either he just pretended they never happened or he was told to press on.

Sgt. Shaw was also forced to admit she never interviewed Sgt. Thomas Andersen, but she tried to play it off and said she couldn't remember whom she had interviewed. Andersen was a member of the Organized Crime Unit, which worked closely with VOTF officers and agents, so naturally Andersen would fall under my command. Shaw made sure she didn't talk to everyone on the VOTF or the Organized Crime Unit, because a few of them made it clear they would not cover up any misconduct. Andersen was one of those honorable officers. In my mind, Shaw wanted nothing to do with Andersen or any other honest cop.

Attorney Albert Goins went after Sergeant Shaw full throttle, and within minutes Shaw looked as if she had run a marathon. The smug look she had come in with was gone. The stress of testifying under oath and knowing she could not go toe-to-toe with a highly skilled veteran attorney only made it worse. Goins was a brilliant man who chewed up Shaw and her attorney. In my eyes, Nelson was no match for Goins, and I believe he knew it. So he fought him tooth and nail even when there was no need to fight. Nelson's only chance of winning this case was to put his career and liberty on the line. The case was over. Sgt. Burt had come forward. A highly respected FBI agent, Michelle O'Shea, and an equally highly respected assistant US attorney, Nancy Hanson, backed up Burt, and Burt backed me up. But Nelson knew the FBI would not let their agents and attorneys testify, so his only chance to win the case would be during summary judgment.

(Summary judgment is when the attorneys from both parties argue the merits of the case before the judge and then he or she decides whether the case can proceed to trial.)

Sgt. Shaw did her best to avoid Goins's jabs, but she was slowly getting knocked out. Shaw tried to be coy, but Goins only pursued her harder as she quoted Officer Hardy's Internal Affairs report, in which he claimed I compromised a Title 3 wiretap by tipping off the Faribault police chief and Rice County sheriff without authorization. Shaw had been destroyed, and she looked like a lost kid looking for her Mom. It was game over, but Goins had one last question to knock out Shaw. He noted that on October 5, 2007, the decision was made that there would be no investigation of what I believed was Officer Hardy's false statement.

Goins then quoted Shaw's statement that the FBI allegedly told her I was not going to be accused of that misdeed because it never happened. Shaw replied, "Exactly."

Goins followed up with, "What about the accusation which appears to be patently false as made by Off. Hardy?"

"There was no follow up on that," Shaw answered.

Goins shot back: "The question I have for you, is why?"

After a very long pause, and staring at the ceiling for what seemed like an eternity, Sgt. Shaw finally replied, "I don't have an answer."

Perhaps the most important thing to note here, considering the totality of the circumstances, was that the lead attorney for the City of Minneapolis (Nelson) was sitting right next to Sgt. Shaw. MPD policy seemed to dictate that Officer Hardy should have been relieved of duty, terminated, and charged, but Shaw did none of the above. I believed Shaw was negligent and complicit in criminal misconduct. She had seemingly turned a blind eye to an officer who appeared to have tried to frame me, and the lead Minneapolis assistant city attorney, David Nelson, was sitting right next to Sgt. Shaw as she was forced to confess. In no uncertain terms, Shaw confessed there never was an investigation of the phony cover story that was the backbone of the corruption. If Shaw had drafted paperwork to fire Hardy and those who corroborated his story, everything would have come to a screeching halt in late 2007 or early 2008.

As bad as it all was during Shaw's first deposition, there was still more to come. Little did I and my attorneys know that Shaw and the MPD were sitting on evidence that would corroborate virtually everything I had been saying since day one. The city of Minneapolis and its police department were acting with deliberate indifference. Shaw likely knew of Sgt. Burt's 2010 Internal Affairs complaint when she gave her first deposition in 2011, but she never once mentioned it. Remember: this was an Internal Affairs investigator presumably dedicated to law and order.

Later in the day, my attorneys deposed Lieutenant Raymond Hanssen after they finished with Shaw for the day. I wasn't impressed with Hanssen as a cop or a person. Hanssen was assigned to the computer forensic unit, and he was allegedly recruited by VOTF officers to purge my city computer for one, and only one, reason—to erase an apology to me from ATF supervisor Gary Pedowski. Hanssen may have been used by the cops, because he seemingly had no clue what they were doing. I don't think Hanssen erased the email, but somebody did when VOTF officers had my city computer open.

The pretext for purging my computer was that I was talking to the media. I was being hounded by local reporter Caroline Lowe, of WCCO-TV, and Paul McEnroe, of the *Star Tribune*, but the records were very clear that Lowe repeatedly called me and I only returned one phone call. I never talked to McEnroe until years later, after the Roberts trial. The police union eventually convinced me to give Lowe a sit-down interview, but I never revealed to her anything about the operations of the VOTF.

A few months later, a high-ranking Minneapolis police union official was deposed, and he quickly confirmed that Maj. Yates offered me my rank back shortly after he and Deputy Chief Parker took it in the fall of 2009. So why did they take it in the first place if they were going give it back? Apparently to shut me up. Furthermore, Maj. Yates also told me one day when I ran into him at city hall that he would give me back my rank. Yates would tell a much different story years later in 2017, as he obviously forgot about his conversations with me and the union representative.

CHAPTER 9
THE MISSING TAPE

In the spring of 2011, my lawyers ordered Capt. Hess back for his second deposition. He had been called into Judge Rau's chambers and compelled to tell him why he had sat down with assistant city attorney Lyon, Deputy Chief Parker, and Maj. Wagner to discuss my April 2010 Internal Affairs complaint against Parker, Wagner, and others. Nobody knows what Hess told Judge Rau, but I suspect he did everything possible to cover himself and everyone else.

Hess was scared when he sat down. I could see it on his face, but he tried to act calm. He quickly admitted Deputy Chief Parker and Maj. Wagner were suspects in my third Internal Affairs complaint, and they were also the judge and jury of that complaint against them. Attorney Albert Goins didn't have to push Hess this time, but he did play dumb when he was forced to admit he knew that Chief Dolan and Deputy Chief Parker had farmed out at least two other cases to the FBI, but not this case. I thought that if he had any courage or integrity, he should have demanded it. Nevertheless, Hess confirmed I wanted an outside agency to conduct a criminal probe of the MPD, and he conceded internal affairs investigators are not allowed to give suspects details about a case, but that seems to be exactly what they did.

Capt. Hess went further and conceded he was being directed by Parker and Wagner on how to run the investigation. Hess, it seemed to me, was deliberately conducting a sloppy "investigation" intentionally designed to fail. "I was speaking to the persons accused of wrongdoing," he conceded, and he went even further. "The accused in this case, my supervisors, had an interest in the case." Hess sounded like a robot. That wasn't cop talk; that was lawyer talk. I suspect Judge Rau, or someone else, might have told Hess to make that exact statement, word for word.

Attorney Goins jumped on that and said, "In not being found to have committed wrongdoing, correct?" Hess quickly replied, "Correct." Hess was scared and running for cover.

It was almost as if Hess were reading a confession. He said he did not know the City of Minneapolis and the State of Minnesota had conflict-of-interest policies; I didn't believe that for one minute. But he was quick to admit he was ordered to close my 2010 Internal Affairs complaint after meeting with Deputy Chief Parker, Maj. Wagner, and assistant city attorney Lyon.

Finally, Hess was given the question I couldn't wait for. In no uncertain terms, Hess said it was Maj. Wagner who had told him not to give me a Garrity warning. I had given Hess a detailed nine-page complaint in April of 2010 and later a nineteen-page statement. In the reports, I outlined the phone calls to the reporters with pinpoint detail, the city hall attack, Shaw's alleged misconduct for not seeking Hardy's termination, and several other potential crimes. He had plenty of evidence to launch an investigation, but I believe Deputy Chief Parker and Maj. Wagner wanted more information for one, and only one, reason—to spit hairs on some little detail so they could frame me. I had given them more than enough information to indict several officers, but Capt. Hess said his superiors still wanted more. When I, based on the advice of my attorneys and the union, refused, Deputy Chief Parker and his cronies quickly shut the case down under the guise that I wasn't cooperating. I made them show their cards, and they lost no matter what they did. In my opinion, my nine-page and nineteen-page statements are irrefutable evidence of overwhelming criminal misconduct that can never be erased. They are part of the official record. A federal grand jury would have a field day with my statements and Sgt. Burt's statements to Internal Affairs.

Once again, the case should have immediately been farmed out to another agency. There should have been a parallel MPD Internal Affairs investigation conducted by a neutral MPD investigator issuing compelled Garrity statements when necessary, which would have been standard operating procedure, but they did nothing.

Attorney Goins was on a roll, and in the spring of 2011, he deposed Sgt. Gemma Shaw for the second time. This second deposition was more fireworks. Goins and Ward set Shaw up for the kill. They brought up Shaw's story, claiming I said officers were being indicted. Shaw's eyes said it all; she seemed frightened. Shaw was literally trembling, and then Goins let her have it when he demanded a tape and a printout of the call between her and me. Shaw had completely forgotten she had told Sgt. Zabel she taped the call but the tape recorder allegedly malfunctioned. In an absolute panic, she blurted out that she never taped the call because she called me on her cell phone. Wow! Just like that, she cracked under pressure and came up with a new version. Goins tore into her big-time. Shaw had now created a bigger mess and Goins was having a field day. He now had two stories. Goins ripped her to shreds and made her settle on which story she was going with today, the tape malfunction story or the story that there never was a tape because she used her cell phone. Shaw, looking bewildered and shocked, decided to go with her original story about the tape recorder malfunctioning.

Goins moved on and got Shaw to admit she did preinterviews without a tape recorder. That's how she selected the right officers to back up Officer Hardy and his allies, who corroborated the infamous cover story. It seemed to me to be a blatant violation of department policy. But who was behind the cover story? Hardy relayed it to Internal Affairs, but who was the architect? Was it the Minneapolis FBI or the Minnesota US attorney? The MPD command staff? Was it a team effort, or were VOTF officers so desperate for overtime they would do or say anything? It's a question that most likely can only be answered through a massive federal investigation.

In the summer of 2011, Carter Reed was deposed for the first time. Goins wasted no time ripping Reed to shreds. He was vague and maybe even deceitful, and Goins threatened to call the US magistrate and compel him to come clean. He constantly kept looking at his attorney, Tim Boone, for answers until Boone finally got annoyed enough to tell him to stop. All he had to do was honestly answer the questions.

Reed said my opinion that VOTF officers could be indicted was not improper if it was true, but Yates led him to believe I made a false statement and was "disruptive." Furthermore, Maj. Yates allegedly never told Reed what the so-called disruption was, and Reed allegedly never asked him. I didn't believe that for one minute. Nevertheless, Reed admitted he had no evidence or facts that I was ever disruptive. So essentially he succumbed to allowing his boss to keep me from exposing internal corruption to an outside law enforcement agency. By his own admission, he never objected to anything.

Reed also told Goins that assistant city attorney Tilly Heck helped him write the performance improvement plan in September 2009. Reed tried to have it both ways, but it was futile. Throwing Tilly Heck under the bus didn't help him. He signed the PIP, and he can't deny it. The facts were irrefutable, and there was a paper trail to corroborate everything. He further discredited himself when he said I had been given annual performance reports. No such reports were ever drafted after I was demoted in 2009, because I was consistently outperforming my peers with successful criminal complaints. In 2010 and 2011, I outperformed my peers with sixty more criminal complaints than other detectives in my unit, and the MPD did not want that documented.

Reed claimed that he had no idea why I was demoted and that Maj. Yates allegedly never told him why. Only a fool would believe such nonsense. Regardless, Reed did admit that if I had gone outside the MPD or talked to the mayor, I would have violated the PIP. In other words, my free speech was seemingly restricted by my employer, the MPD, and I would have been fired if I had violated the PIP.

Reed seemed to be doing his best to blame everyone else. Police supervisors write reports and evaluations all the time, and yet he needed an attorney for a simple, routine performance improvement plan. Was he incompetent, or was he so deeply involved in putting a gag order on a whistleblower that he needed the help of an attorney? Furthermore, why was Major Wesley Yates involved in such a simple matter?

Remember: Yates was sitting right next to Parker in the summer of 2007 when Deputy Chief Parker admitted to me the FBI wanted me removed from my command. Yates should have known I was just doing my job, and he also should have known the PIP was nothing more than an illegal gag order regardless of who was behind it. Not only that, but Sgt. Zabel's Internal Affairs investigation confirmed I never spread any rumors or was in any way disruptive.

Reed seemed to be in serious trouble. Just seven months earlier, he and Maj. Wagner were alleging that VOTF officers repeatedly miscarried. Yet now he was pretending that everything was just a "management oversight issue" and that he was in a fog about the PIP. Reed had previously claimed multiple allegations of potential criminal misconduct involving some VOTF officers, and Goins forced him to admit there was no follow-up Internal Affairs investigation or a criminal probe.

Reed testified that FBI agent O'Shea, assistant US attorney Hanson, and MPD Internal Affairs sergeant Bill Mason told him there were serious problems inside the task force. Reed said Mason and O'Shea told him some VOTF officers selected cases based on how much overtime money they could make. Some VOTF officers were making well over $40,000 a year in overtime alone, and he said he had no doubt they were motivated by lucrative overtime.

Goins asked him, "Did you identify a specific assistant US attorney who believed some VOTF officers were manipulative and untruthful?" Reed replied, "Yes." Reed went on to say it was his understanding that the federal partners felt the MPD was turning a blind eye to the misconduct. Besides recommending new officers and supervisors, he did absolutely nothing. Reed also said the FBI told him some VOTF officers were using wiretaps to increase overtime and abusing their discretion with informants.

That's what I said back in 2007. Let's not forget about the bad informant who led VOTF officers to an innocent family's home in

December 2007. There was no legitimate internal or external investigation of the VOTF then either. Finally, Capt. Reed also confirmed there was no investigation of the missing $12,000 as outlined in Sgt. Burt's 2010 Internal Affairs complaint.

The message seemed to be crystal clear to the rank-and-file officers in the MPD. If you had friends in the front office, you had absolute impunity to do whatever you wanted.

In the fall of 2011, Sgt. Burt was deposed. Burt was assigned to the DEA Task Force. Perhaps the most alarming aspect of Burt's Internal Affairs complaint was that the city and the police department knew about it in the spring of 2010 but seemingly kept it from me and my attorneys. Were they hoping we would never discover it? Were they hiding it? It came to light only after Burt and I ran into each other in the fall of 2011, almost a year and a half after he made the complaint. During his deposition, Sgt. Burt said he made his complaint to Sgt. Mason in early 2010. Mason and Shaw were good friends, and I suspect Mason may have helped Shaw try to cover her tracks. I also suspect Mason may have misled FBI agent O'Shea and assistant US attorney Hanson by embellishing VOTF misconduct to take pressure off Shaw, but that's only my assumption.

At any rate, this was bad news for Shaw and the MPD, because I now had backup in the form of a well-known and highly respected twenty-six-year veteran of the force. A highly respected sergeant assigned to the DEA task force blew the whistle, and everything he said mirrored what I had been saying for years. But the Minneapolis police command staff quickly shut down Burt's complaint, according to Capt. Huffman, without initiating a routine Internal Affairs investigation.

Sgt. Burt provided Internal Affairs with twelve pages outlining potential crimes and misconduct, but the MPD didn't want to hear any of it. When questioned about this, Capt. Hess said he could not open an internal investigation unless Maj. Wagner approved it. He was the Internal Affairs director. It was his job to launch an investigation. I don't believe he needed the approval of his supervisor. I believe he was not being honest. Every complaint alleging potential criminal misconduct by police officers must be investigated. In fact, it was bullet point 1 of Deputy Chief Parker's April 2009 propaganda letter: "We will vigorously investigate any and all allegations of corruption. There is no acceptable degree of corruption in law enforcement."

Sgt. Burt's only other complaint to Internal Affairs in his twenty-six years was against a cop who stole money. Sgt. Burt said he called Internal Affairs ten to fifteen times before he was told his case was shut down. I believe the officers mentioned in Burt's complaint should have been relieved of duty and suspended. There should have been multiple search warrants and subpoenas issued for the missing ICE funds, the VOTF overtime account fund, and several other issues Burt exposed, including the nearly $300,000 pulled away from the City of Chicago. This is not to mention the question, Who were the officers that used up all that seized money? Was using seized money from drug dealers to directly fund officers' overtime even legal?

Before Sgt. Burt testified, he requested that my lawyers send him a subpoena because he feared retaliation for testifying. Burt told me and my lawyers that Captain Heidi Kirby called him up screaming and swearing for getting the MPD's narcotics unit and the DEA involved in a case VOTF was investigating. Burt tried to explain the need for a bilingual officer in the case, but Kirby didn't seem to care. It was all about seizing money from the case, and she didn't want to share it with the MPD narcotics unit or the DEA. Shortly thereafter, VOTF officers seized $50,000 from the case and put it into a VOTF overtime account. The DEA was outraged and immediately quit working with VOTF.

Sgt. Burt said VOTF lacked diversity, and he told the FBI that VOTF officers were unethical and abusing overtime—exactly what I had said in 2007. Burt also said VOTF investigated a prostitution case even though none of the suspects were violent offenders. But the case offered a lot of overtime surveillance, and that's what he believed motivated VOTF. Burt said that between twenty and thirty cops felt the same way he did. Think about it; Burt said that between twenty and thirty cops felt the same way he did.

Burt told Goins he told Sgt. Mason that he felt Officers Hardy,

Speer, Baker, Denton, and Evans were bad cops and should be removed from the task force. It's no coincidence that I believe that all of these officers nudged the FBI to remove me from my command back in 2007 so they could allegedly collect unaccountable overtime.

Burt said VOTF's main objective was making money. Sgt. Burt said the DEA, ICE, and the ATF quit working with VOTF officers because they were unethical. Sergeant Burt said good VOTF officers like Officers Eck and Beiderman were afraid to speak out because they believed they would face retaliation. Burt also said Capt. Kirby was untouchable.

Burt said a high-ranking commander, most likely Kirby, set up an overtime seizure account after I was forced out. Burt said I never had or would allow such an account. Burt said that wiretaps were set up to expand overtime and that many were, in his mind, completely unjustified. There was never an investigation of anything, so nobody even knows for certain if it was even legal to take seized drug money and use it to directly pay cops overtime. Seizures are supposed to go through the city accountant's office, but it's unclear whether that ever happened.

Burt said he never heard anyone ever complain about me. He said a few select VOTF officers claimed they worked on the weekend and that is how $12,000 was allegedly removed from an ICE account—something that the police department command staff refused to investigate. Several officers believe the department knows who took it, but they won't do anything because the suspects might be Parker's friends. Burt said city accountant Lily Theis never complained about me. She told Burt that Minneapolis Police Captain Kirby tried to put $200,000 from a seized FBI account into the VOTF overtime account, but she stopped it. Finally, Sgt. Burt said I was the victim of a "smear campaign."

Sgt. Paul Burt's deposition was a relief for me and my lawyers. Attorney Goins would later say it was so nice to depose an honest cop who didn't play games—no "I don't recall" games, no "I don't remember" games. He was just a very decent and honorable police officer telling the truth.

In the fall of 2011, VOTF officer Denton was deposed for the first time under federal court jurisdiction. Attorney Albert Goins, like attorney Marshall Tanick in a previous state court deposition, wasted no time going after Officer Denton, and Denton wasted no time denying he was one of *Star Tribune* reporter David Chanen's sources—this despite detailed cell phone evidence linking him to Chanen's office phone as Chanen worked on the story about me in May 2009, just before the start of the Roberts trial on May 11. Officer Denton repeatedly said, "I don't recall" and "I have no recollection," but he was forced to admit he made well over $40,000 in overtime in 2008 as a member of VOTF.

CHAPTER 10
INTERNAL AFFAIRS CORRUPTION

CALLING ME INTO INTERNAL AFFAIRS IN THE SUMMER OF 2008 AS A witness in the Capt. Crawford case was nothing but a ruse to see whether I had a tape of Jackson lying or any assistant US attorney warnings. So when Sergeant Gemma Shaw was deposed, Attorney Goins asked her whether Speer, Hardy, Baker, Denton, Wright, or Evans ever asked her to ask me whether I had a tape of my interview with Jackson, and Shaw replied, "I don't think so." "I don't think so" was the wrong answer. You see, in Shaw's mind, if any of them ever flipped and cooperated with the government, Shaw could say she wasn't lying, but just didn't think so. She should have replied with an emphatic "No!"

Goins kept up the pressure and asked her whether anyone ever asked her whether I taped my interview with Jackson. She replied, "I don't remember that ever coming up." Once again, right there Shaw was seemingly not conforming to the truth. That was the whole reason for calling me into Internal Affairs in the first place. They wanted to know whether I had a tape of Jackson lying about the officers he claimed were corrupt, and they seemed to have used Capt. Crawford's Internal Affairs case seemed to be a ruse to bring me into Internal Affairs and give a compelled Garrity statement. The powers that be were more than willing to demand a compelled statement from me when it benefited them. They had no choice. They had to know before they could indict Roberts, and Shaw was likely in on all of it from start to finish. If they indicted Roberts and I produced a tape, the house would fall. The million-dollar question remains: who was the attorney who coached Shaw?

Remember: the police administration allegedly did not want a compelled Garrity-protected statement from me when I made my third Internal Affairs complaint, because it would have prevented the city from framing me, but they seemingly had no problem demanding I give them a compelled Garrity-protected statement to see whether I had evidence that they were covering up evidence. Funny how that worked for the powers that be in Minneapolis.

Goins pressed on and asked Sgt. Shaw if the FBI ever asked her whether I had a tape of my interview of Jackson. Now she emphatically replied, "No!" Right there and then, my attorneys and I knew the FBI was most likely not directly involved in the collusion surrounding the Internal Affairs debacle. They could still be behind everything, but nobody from the FBI asked Shaw; that was clear. The FBI could have used a VOTF cop to do their dirty work, but according to Shaw, nobody from the FBI asked her. The FBI wasn't that dumb. Every FBI agent and attorney involved in this massive case knew damn well that asking Shaw to call me into Internal Affairs under pretext to go fishing for proof that I had evidence that they were covering up evidence—Jackson's false statements or assistant US attorney warnings—was not only improper; it was most likely criminal.

It could have been that Shaw was covering for the FBI, or that they were not at all involved in that very dangerous ruse, or that they used a VOTF cop to get the job done. Remember: Shaw never provided the name of the FBI agent she claimed told her the cover story was baseless nonsense. Sgt. Shaw seemed afraid of the FBI, and she was so rattled at this point that she looked as if she could collapse. She played the "I don't think so," "I don't remember" game when fellow Minneapolis cops were mentioned, but her memory suddenly became crystal clear when the FBI was mentioned. The cops, agents, and attorneys did a lot of stupid things throughout this horrific ordeal, but it's interesting that there are no FBI names linked to the cover story or the dirty deed of ordering me into Internal Affairs to see whether I had a tape of Jackson lying and assistant

US attorneys warning cops and FBI agents the case would be shut down if Jackson lied. These two key elements—no FBI names linked to the cover story, and my compelled internal affairs statement before Officer Roberts was indicted—are extremely important. Criminal defense attorneys believe these two elements are an important link to identifying the culpable parties in a seemingly well designed case of conspiracy to obstruct justice and a whole lot more.

Shaw once again had a memory lapse when she was asked whether she ever went back and told VOTF officers I did not have any recording. She said, "I don't recall." Sensing that Shaw might be untruthful, Goins jumped on that and asked Shaw whether she could dispute that she did. Shaw said, "I don't believe I did that."

It was very clear in my mind that Shaw was not conforming to the truth. Goins asked her whether she had shared a copy of my statement with anyone from VOTF. Once again Shaw had a remarkable memory and adamantly said no. Shaw's mind was going one hundred miles an hour—I could see it in her eyes—and just like that, she changed her answer. Without any pushing or prodding from Goins, Shaw blurted out that my statement was available to everyone in the MPD chain of command. Shaw knew that a competent and ethical Internal Affairs investigation would easily be able to identify anyone who had printed the statement or pulled it up on his or her computer. I believe Shaw has a lot more to tell, but it will only happen if she is charged or indicted.

That volley of questions and answers made it clear to me and my attorneys that there was likely collusion between Shaw, VOTF, and attorneys. Goins kept pressing Shaw and asked her directly whether she had shared the results of my statement with anyone from the US attorney's office. Shaw should have emphatically said no, just as she had when she was asked about the FBI, but she didn't. **One could have heard a pin drop. Everyone knew right there and then that the US attorney's office was likely involved.**

Shaw's answer was "I don't believe I did." Once again, it was the wrong answer! It was all attorney Goins needed. He had done a spectacular job. Shaw was humiliated and exposed, big time.

This is an extremely important point and must be reiterated. Shaw was adamant she had no direct involvement with the FBI regarding my compelled Internal Affairs statement in 2008 before Roberts was indicted, but she never cleared VOTF cops or any assistant US attorneys of their involvement. This is seemingly a weak link in the culpable parties' game plan regarding conspiracy to obstruct justice and would offer a future criminal probe a great deal of power and latitude in dividing the culpable players and turning them against one another.

In the spring of 2012, Maj. Wagner was deposed for the first time. Wagner was like a racehorse blasting out of the gate, but she never imagined I would get my hands on Sgt. Burt's March 2010 Internal Affairs complaint.

I thought Wagner was no angel in any of this, so Goins and Ward set Wagner up and asked her what her opinion of Sgt. Burt was. Wagner replied, "He's a good, very good officer." Just like that, Goins had Wagner on the ropes. Wagner had sent me a letter a few months before this deposition threatening to terminate me and accusing me of making false statements, likely knowing full well this "very good officer" had backed me up completely. Ward glanced over at Goins, and the fireworks began. Goins wasted no time letting Wagner know we knew about Sgt. Burt's March 2010 Internal Affairs complaint, and with that Wagner looked as if she wanted to cry. She was totally caught off guard. She had no idea my attorneys and I knew about it. She was in shock and had nowhere to turn.

Wagner must have quickly realized she was no match for Goins and Ward, so she pretty much conceded. Goins had Wagner on her heels so fast she never knew what hit her, and she was clearly shaken. Without hesitation, Wagner tried to cover herself and said, "I forwarded that on to Deputy Chief Parker," referring to Sgt. Burt's complaint.

When Goins demanded to know what Deputy Chief Parker said when she gave him the report, Wagner looked over at assistant city attorney Boone for help. But Boone was stone-faced. Goins seemed to make Wagner all the more nervous with his deep voice and confidence. Wagner seemed literally scared out of her mind. Wagner said that Deputy

Chief Parker told her, "I get what I need from VOTF." Wagner quickly rephrased her answer and said that Parker told her, "I'm happy with what I get from VOTF."

In a panic, Wagner just told Goins, in no uncertain terms, that a deputy Minneapolis chief of police essentially told her the ends justified the means after she gave him Sgt. Burt's detailed complaint about corruption from a highly respected twenty-plus-year veteran of the force. I believed Wagner herself wasn't innocent. She threatened to fire me, likely knowing full well that everything Sgt. Burt was alleging corroborated everything I had been saying. Throwing Parker under the bus didn't help her one bit.

Wagner went on to tell the lawyers she never met with Sgt. Burt, and she denied she ever told Internal Affairs Captain Jerry Hess to shut Burt's case down. But Hess said she did. Hess had nothing to lose by pointing the finger at Wagner; she was his boss. But Wagner seemingly had everything to lose, because shutting down Burt's case was wrong, and likely criminal. Burt outlined a number of potential crimes.

Goins pressed on and asked Wagner about Burt's concerns of racism, and Wagner admitted that racism justified an Internal Affairs investigation. As soon as Wagner admitted to that, Goins asked her about my third Internal Affairs complaint, in April 2010. Wagner said she had no recollection of my third Internal Affairs complaint, which addressed the bogus PIP, the city hall attack, the infamous cover story, FBI misconduct, the media attacks, her threat to terminate me, and my notification to Internal Affairs that I had another officer who was willing to come forward. At the time, I had no knowledge Sgt. Burt had already come forward, so this was now a third officer, Sgt. Andersen, who was willing to step up and address misconduct and racism inside the task force.

Wagner arrogantly said my claims were "unsubstantiated," but she did admit to meeting with Deputy Chief Parker, Captain Jerry Hess, and assistant city attorney Ernest Lyon regarding my complaint, which listed both Parker and her as potential suspects. What was going on here? First she had no recollection of my complaint, and now she admitted to having a meeting about it. The only reason Burt's, Andersen's, and my claims were "unsubstantiated" was because Wagner and Parker refused to conduct a full-scale internal investigation in concert with a neutral outside criminal investigation by another agency.

Three veteran white male supervisors with exemplary records came forward and exposed corruption and racism, only to be cast aside and counteraccused. The message to the bad apples in the rank and file was clear: You can do whatever the hell you want. We've got your back.

Major Anna Wagner seemed to be walking herself right into the middle of criminal misconduct. Goins went after her full throttle for allegedly ordering Capt. Hess to shut down my 2010 Internal Affairs complaint, according to Hess, but Wagner denied she gave such an order. So up to this point, Wagner was accused of shutting down Burt's Internal Affairs complaint and my third Internal Affairs complaint, according to Capt. Hess.

So just to recap, my first Internal Affairs complaint was about VOTF misconduct and the infamous cover story in the fall of 2007, after I was removed from my command. My second Internal Affairs complaint was in the summer of 2009 regarding Shaw's manufactured evidence: her statements to Wagner and the FBI about "sealed indictments." My third Internal Affairs complaint was in the spring of 2010 regarding the media attacks, the city hall attack, and other misconduct. Two of my three Internal Affairs complaints, like Sgt. Burt's Internal Affairs complaint, were shut down. Only my 2009 Internal Affairs complaint was investigated by Sgt. Zabel, but because the MPD commanders didn't like the outcome, they seemingly just ignored it and all the evidence. Malfeasance was the name of the game, and nobody was held accountable. Doomsday for the MPD was inevitable.

Wagner was not handling the hot seat well. In a seeming panic, she screwed up again just as before and said that her understanding of the meeting was that Capt. Hess was supposed to proceed, but then she quickly did an about-face and said she had no specific recollection of the meeting's directive before once again making another about-face and claiming Hess should have continued with the investigation. It was like Ping-Pong. Back and forth. Which story was she going to go with?

Goins sensed Wagner was once again falling apart, so he showed her the evidence. Wagner now admitted she had received all of my memos and statements from Capt. Hess. This was another bombshell. Maj. Wagner, like Deputy Chief Parker, were suspects in my third Internal Affairs complaint, and now Wagner was claiming Hess had shown her the evidence. The Internal Affairs director, Captain Jerry Hess, had allegedly tipped off his boss, Major Anna Wagner! Hess and Wagner seemed to have now officially turned on each other.

Wagner had now evened the score and seemed to have thrown Hess under the bus, but she was also squarely putting herself in the middle of likely collusion. Goins was amazed by Wagner's statements, thinking perhaps Wagner didn't realize she was shooting herself in the foot. Goins pressed on, and Wagner confirmed she was named as a suspect in my third Internal Affairs complaint, and at that point, the light went on in Wagner's head. She had just confessed to a wide range of potential criminal misconduct. Wagner was so out of control emotionally she didn't realize that when she admitted that Hess tipped her off, they were both in the same boat.

If my case had been farmed out, Wagner and Parker would have been questioned by an unknown officer, and they would never have seen any evidence against them.

Attorney Goins brought up the Garrity warning, which insulates officers from criminal prosecution when they give compelled statements. It's designed in part to encourage whistleblowers to come forward. Goins asked Maj. Wagner about the Garrity warning, and Wagner seemed to start to admit she told Capt. Hess not to give one to me. But then she said, "I don't remember." More Ping-Pong.

The police union had wanted Capt. Hess to give me a Garrity warning, but I believe Hess refused, so I just gave my statement anyway. I really didn't care either way, because I had done nothing wrong. That's why I gave Hess a nineteen-page, non-Garrity statement in addition to my initial nine-page complaint. I had no doubt in my mind they were doing everything they could to discourage me from coming forward. They wanted me to disappear.

After Maj. Wagner said, "I don't remember," she blurted out, "I don't order people." Moments later she said, "There were no orders given to anybody." Wagner went on to say that no decision was made by the police department not to give me a Garrity warning. Wagner was all over the map. Goins quickly reminded Wagner that Capt. Hess had already told them that was not only not true but also that Wagner was the one who gave him the order not to give me a Garrity warning.

Wagner, knowing she was pinned again, said, "That's fine; if that was my decision, I'm okay with that." Goins stared at Wagner and demanded more, and at that point Wagner seemed to panic and changed her story again. She said, "I don't characterize it as an option per se, but there was no order ever given to Jerry [Capt. Hess] to do so." Wagner's bizarre behavior continued, and once again she changed her story, this time saying it was a "mutual decision" not to give me a Garrity warning. She continued to deny that she directed the investigation, despite Hess's statement that she did. Nobody wanted to take ownership of shutting down massive Internal Affairs cases and refusing to give whistleblowers the Garrity warning to protect them from false counterclaims by corrupt officers.

My attorneys and I were amazed that Wagner kept changing her story, and it didn't stop. True to form, Wagner once again changed her story. Now she claimed Hess was supposed to continue with the investigation, including a Garrity warning, but she denied saying she told Hess to take a Garrity statement from me. It was unbelievable! I sent a note across the table to my attorneys: "She needs to be medicated!" Both attorneys smiled and called for a break in the deposition. It was obvious Wagner was losing it.

When the deposition resumed, Maj. Wagner finally admitted she told Capt. Hess not to give me a Garrity warning. Boone must have convinced her to just tell the truth during the break. After all that drama, Wagner finally came clean.

Near the end of her deposition, Goins forced Wagner to admit she had seen my nine-page April 29, 2010, letter to Internal Affairs director Capt. Hess outlining how Wright's and Denton's city cell phones showed calls to Chanen. Wagner's admission that Hess showed her the document once again put Wagner in the middle of potential wrongdoing. Wagner may have thought she was getting even with Hess, and she was to an extent, but she also seemed to be confessing to collaborating with Hess. Capt. Hess had a legal obligation to keep that document and all the evidence out of the hands of the suspects, but apparently he had shared it with one of them: Maj. Wagner.

Moreover, Wagner confirmed she read my very detailed April 2010 internal affairs complaint, so she knew that she and Deputy Chief Parker were listed as suspects. Wagner never recused herself. It was all about self-preservation.

Goins wisely decided this was now a good time to bring up Wagner's seemingly threatening letter. Wagner immediately denied writing the letter and said an assistant city attorney wrote it. Wagner couldn't wait to throw the unknown attorney under the bus, but she was forced to admit she signed it, and by signing it she was forced to accept ownership. Once again Wagner put herself right back in the middle. Attorney Boone would not allow Wagner to identify the attorney. The letter made it perfectly clear my third Internal Affairs complaint was closed, and I could see Wagner was trying to control herself, but inside she seemed to be raging with anger. She knew she was in another no-win situation, and Goins was winding up to deliver more stunning blows to a woman who seemed to be on the verge of a complete and total loss of physical and emotional control. Goins went right for the jugular and asked her one more time whether she had ordered Capt. Hess to shut down my April 2010 Internal Affairs complaint. She said, "I might have."

Apparently she forgot she had already confessed to it.

CHAPTER 11
MINNEAPOLIS COP CRACKS UNDER PRESSURE

IN THE SPRING OF 2012, OFFICER NICK EVANS WAS DEPOSED. Evans tried to play the role of a tough guy, but he seemed weak and insecure. Goins was ripping Evans to shreds for all his nonsense, and within no time, in a panic, he threw assistant US attorney Henry Stahl under the bus. Evans made everyone's jaw drop when he told Goins that Stahl had tipped him off about my top-secret US Department of Justice inspector general complaint! The initial reaction was one of absolute shock. There was dead silence. *Did he just say that?* I wondered. *Yes, he did.* Evans, in no uncertain terms, potentially just laid out a Title 18 case of criminal conspiracy and a whole lot more—maybe a RICO case. It was absolutely golden. All the anger I felt when looking at Evans dissipated when he gave up Stahl. It was an absolute game-changer. Evans's disclosure was the equivalent of a nuclear bomb.

Evans provided details and told Goins that Stahl had tipped him and Officer Denton off about my confidential, top-secret US Department of Justice inspector general complaint. Only myself, attorney Fred Bruno, and Sheriff Stanek had knowledge of my confidential complaint. However, the inspector general's office "accidentally" sent my confidential complaint to FBI SSA agent Irving in Minneapolis instead of FBI Inspections in Washington, DC, and presumably somebody in the Minneapolis FBI field office or the Chicago inspector general's office tipped off Stahl, and Stahl tipped off the cops. Evans laid out a potential criminal conspiracy under the color of law within a matter of minutes.

It was an extremely serious allegation, and we knew it was true. SSA Irving should have immediately sent the complaint to FBI Inspections in Washington DC, but instead he sent me a letter and requested a meeting. Irving, or someone from the Minneapolis FBI office, or someone from the Chicago field office of the IG, shared it with assistant US attorney Stahl and perhaps several others. None of this would have ever been known if not for the deposition.

According to Evans, assistant US attorney Stahl tipped him off, and Denton as well. Obviously they all needed to be on the same page because the inspector general and I were seemingly coming after them. They were playing with fire, and the apparent mistakes were piling up fast.

The thought of me testifying in Roberts's case seemed to scare everyone involved. Covering up exculpatory evidence is big-time police corruption, and the criminal penalties for law enforcement officers doing so under the color of law are extremely harsh. In no uncertain terms, somebody in the Minneapolis FBI field office or the inspector general's office tipped off Stahl, and Stahl allegedly tipped off the cops according to Officer Evans's sworn testimony. **All of this could lead to federal indictments of attorneys and law enforcement officers, if handled properly.**

Evans's testimony was earth-shaking, and everything fit. If everything happened as my attorneys and I suspect, VOTF officers, under the guidance of an assistant US attorney, recruited Sgt. Shaw to call me into Internal Affairs under the guise that I was a witness in Capt. Crawford's Internal Affairs case. But before the interview was over, Shaw was instructed to ask me whether I had any tape recordings of my interview with Jackson at the FBI safe house or any assistant US attorneys warning cops and FBI agents that the case would immediately be shut down if Jackson lied about anything. Almost a year later, according to Evans, assistant US attorney Stahl told him I turned them all into the US Department of Justice in April 2009. The stakes were high, and everyone involved had to be on the same page.

This revelation was and still is the biggest bombshell in this case. At the very least, it gave us and the Justice Department a Title 18 conspiracy to obstruct

justice claim, but it was more likely a RICO claim involving assistant US attorneys, Minneapolis police officers, and perhaps FBI agents and inspector general agents, and maybe Minneapolis assistant city attorneys if they were involved in this apparently horrific misconduct.

Officer Evans was the weak link I was looking for. My attorneys and I were confident that sooner or later one of the involved officers would break, and sure enough, it happened. Attorney Albert Goins scored a grand slam home run. Officer Evans was pompous when his deposition started, but Goins whipped the cocky smile off his face within minutes.

I felt Assistant US attorney Stahl was one of the most arrogant and sneaky people I had ever met in my law enforcement career, so when Evans told us that Stahl had tipped them off about my inspector general complaint, I wasn't the least bit surprised. This was the guy who called Attorney Fred Bruno and told him he was "this close" to having me arrested.

I couldn't wait for the break so that I could congratulate Albert and Damon. Evans had given us a case for the history books. The bigger question was that of whether the FBI was also directly involved. Clearly somebody inside the Minneapolis FBI office or the Chicago inspector general's office tipped off Stahl, but were these organizations behind the plan to use MPD Internal Affairs to go fishing for evidence that I had tapes of their misconduct? Evans never linked the FBI to anything, but that doesn't mean they were not involved. Assistant city attorney Boone, Evans's attorney, was a stoic man, but when Evans gave up Stahl, it raised Boone's eyebrows. Boone quickly recovered, but I could tell Boone's mind was wandering after that bombshell.

Boone likely knew full well that Evans had just dropped a nuclear bomb, and before it was over, Evans dropped one more crucial bit of information. He admitted he'd heard I had been subpoenaed to testify in the Roberts trial, but he said he didn't know where he'd heard it. How was that possible? The subpoena was sent to Minneapolis assistant city attorney Patrick O'Leary, and from there it went to Deputy Chief Parker. Obviously there was a lot of communication between the city attorney's office, the chief's office, VOTF, and the feds.

In the summer of 2012, Deputy Chief Parker was deposed for the first time. Parker testified that he had no knowledge that the Tre-Tre Crips had threatened to kill a cop in Faribault, and he further testified that he had no knowledge that assistant US attorney Folk had authorized me to brief the Faribault police chief, his captain, and the Rice County sheriff on the basic details of the wiretap. At no point did Parker say he didn't recall or could not remember. He was adamant he had not been told, but I believe I told Parker and Yates most of it during our meeting in August of 2007, though I can't be positive. However, I clearly remember Parker giving up the FBI's request to keep the infamous cover story confidential. Nevertheless, this is extremely important because in 2013 assistant city attorney David Nelson would stand before Judge Doty and swear that MPD commanders could not remember what they were told. Deputy Chief Parker wasn't playing the "I don't recall" game. His memory was clear about what he wanted to remember. Parker was a smart man, but for some unknown reason he gave seemingly blanket immunity to his friends.

It would only get worse for Sgt. Shaw. In the fall of 2012, Maj. Owens also testified that Shaw never told him that I did not violate the wiretap. Eleven days later, it got worse for Shaw when Capt. Robinson backed up Deputy Chief Parker and Maj. Owens when she testified that Shaw never told her that I did not violate the wiretap. Finally, with the lead Minneapolis assistant city attorney, David Nelson, sitting right next to her, Maj. Wagner also testified that Shaw never told her, either. All four commanders testified that Shaw never told them that the "cover story" was a canard. Sgt. Shaw seemingly withheld one of the most crucial pieces of exculpatory evidence from all the commanders—the cover story.

A police Internal Affairs investigator covering up evidence is about as bad as it gets, but remember that Deputy Chief Parker approved removing Sgt. Krebs and Sgt. Denno so that everything could apparently be controlled by Shaw. I have no doubt that VOTF officers recommended Deputy Chief Parker make that move, but it doesn't matter, because Parker and Yates had their opportunity to stop this runaway train the day the FBI marched into Parker's office and asked that I be removed from my command.

The MPD had become an absolute disgrace from the top down, and bad cops were loving every minute of it. Good cops just shook their heads in disgust and kept quiet for fear of losing their jobs and careers. It was an absolute mess, but worse yet, it was a haven for corruption. The message to corrupt cops was clear: you can do whatever you want. Giving bad cops the green light to run wild and do whatever they wanted would eventually bring down the entire MPD.

It was an absolute formula for disaster, and meanwhile the FBI just sat on the sidelines and did nothing. They had no choice, because they had helped create this mess and were deeply involved. My 2009 complaint to the inspector general was eventually sent to the FBI in Washington, DC, but it was obviously thrown up on a shelf or tossed in the garbage, because nothing was ever done. I followed up with three letters to the US Department of Justice Office of Professional Responsibility in October 2010, but again, nothing was done. Retired FBI agent Dan Vogel suspects the reason the FBI did nothing with my case was because the FBI was more obsessed with its image than with holding bad agents accountable.

The FBI was conveniently asleep at the wheel. I believe they knew those two senior FBI agents and their boss had crossed the line when they stabbed me in the back and asked Deputy Chief Parker and Maj. Yates to remove me from my command, and they were not about to let cops testify against FBI agents. FBI agents testify against cops; cops don't testify against FBI agents. The FBI's negligence and misconduct leads many to believe they may have been behind the scam to use Internal Affairs to see whether I had a tape of Jackson's lies and the assistant US attorneys' warnings. The FBI desperately wanted to knock me out so they could relax and let this nightmare end, so maybe they were involved. Only a full-scale criminal investigation can get to the bottom of this colossal mess the FBI helped start. Clearly somebody tipped off Stahl about my confidential inspector general complaint, but who?

As Parker's deposition continued, attorney Albert Goins wasted no time going after Parker and getting him to confirm that he and Chief Dolan had farmed out cases in the past when there had been a conflict of interest. There was nothing Parker could do; he had to admit it. Parker also had to admit being present during the meeting in the spring of 2010 when he, Maj. Wagner, Capt. Hess, and assistant city attorney Ernest Lyon all discussed the evidence against him and Wagner under the guise of "attorney-client privilege." Those two admissions in a court trial might be devastating.

Deputy Chief Parker tried to claim it was a group decision not to investigate my third Internal Affairs complaint. He went further and said the complaint didn't warrant further investigation. Maybe this was because he was a suspect. Parker had no problem launching internal investigations against officers, but the same was seemingly not the case when the investigations would be against him or his friends. Parker then conveniently claimed he did not "recall" seeing or knowing about Maj. Wagner's November 16, 2010, letter threatening me with termination after I made my third Internal Affairs complaint. Parker said he would never have authorized the letter. Parker also denied ever having a conversation about me with reporter David Chanen. If everything he said was true, then why didn't he allow an outside agency to investigate everything so his name could be cleared?

What Parker did not know prior to his deposition was that when I made my third Internal Affairs complaint in April 2010, I left out the fact that I had his cell phone records linking him to Chanen in the days and weeks before the trial. I left that part out because I figured Capt. Hess or someone else would probably tip him off. If Parker had known I had his cell phone records indirectly linking him to Chanen's devastating May 8, 2009, story, I believed he would definitely have shut down the complaint. As it turns out, he did it anyway. I suspected the MPD command staff would cover it up, and they seem to have, but they left a serious paper trail they can never erase.

Regardless, on April 23, 2009, the day after Inspector Gerold asked me for my opinion at a Third Precinct commander's meeting on April

22—the last day of the *Star Tribune* series—Parker called Chanen at 3:37 p.m. The call was for one minute, so perhaps Parker did not get through to Chanen or he left him a message. Five days later, on April 28, at 7:54 a.m., Parker called Chanen again, and this time the call lasted two minutes. Later in the day, Parker called Chanen again at 2:50 p.m., and this call was for three minutes. Parker called Chanen back at 2:53 p.m., and this call was for two minutes. It didn't stop. At 5:00 p.m., Parker called Chanen again, and this call lasted for one minute. Chanen must not have been answering. Parker was persistent, so he called Chanen right back at 5:01 p.m., and again the call was for one minute. Parker was in panic mode. At 5:09 p.m., he called Chanen again, for the sixth time on April 28, and this call was for two minutes. Parker wasn't finished. He seemed to desperately need to get in contact with Chanen, but why? Five o'clock is when the local news starts, but what about newspapers? Was Parker leaking information to television and radio stations via Chanen? At any rate, Parker called Chanen for the seventh time at 5:27 p.m. (after the local news?), and Chanen quickly returned the call. The conversation lasted for five minutes.

A week later, on May 5, Parker called Chanen at 2:55 p.m., and they talked for ten minutes. Three days later, Chanen's article in the *Star Tribune* literally destroyed my career. The first media attack was horrific, but the second media attack, by Minnesota's largest newspaper, was the final nail in the coffin.

The cell phone records of Officer Denton show him repeatedly calling back and forth to Chanen on the evening of May 8, 2009, as Chanen was literally sitting at his desk writing the second media attack. At one point, Capt. Wright was on the phone with Chanen for twelve minutes as Denton was calling, but he obviously received a busy signal. The next day, Evans called Chanen, presumably to congratulate him. Reporter Chanen should be compelled to testify and reveal his sources.

Parker's deposition continued to get odder by the minute, as Parker claimed he didn't remove me from VOTF, stating that he was out of town at the time. Parker also claimed he never knew there was a threat to kill a cop in Faribault. Parker did confirm I told him Jackson was a liar, but then he tried to claim Jackson identified seven officers on the night of his arrest. Parker should have known full well Jackson identified six officers, because I personally briefed Parker and gave him the names of the six Minneapolis police officers.

Parker proceeded to say that if I had talked about or exposed the public corruption case, it would have been a crime. Yet Parker himself likely did just that when he tipped off the Minneapolis police union officials in the fall of 2007, according to his own testimony in a 2008 deposition.

Parker conveniently denied he received or knew about two subpoenas sent to his office demanding my testimony in the Roberts case. Officer Evans was in VOTF, and he knew that I was subpoenaed to testify, and so did Denton, but Deputy Chief Parker did not? Goins had him on the ropes, but Parker knew he had attorney-client privilege with the assistant city attorney or attorneys—most likely Patrick O'Leary—who probably briefed him about the subpoenas.

As the deposition moved along, Goins asked Parker whether he ever talked to any prosecutors before the Roberts trial, and he denied he did, but Parker had no idea that Sgt. Zabel noted in his report that Deputy Chief Parker talked to assistant US attorney Jay Schultz in early May 2009 after Sgt. Shaw spoke about "sealed indictments" pending. Parker called Schultz to check and see whether there were any "sealed indictments" pending. So what if there were sealed indictments? Did the assistant Minneapolis chief of police expect an assistant US attorney to tip him off? What kind of a three-ring circus was going on in Minneapolis? Was every cop, federal agent, and attorney corrupt?

If there were any "sealed indictments," nobody would know about them anyway. That's why they are sealed. There were none. Shaw seemed to make it all up. Nevertheless, per Sgt. Zabel's report, assistant US attorney Schultz checked for indictments and notified Deputy Chief Parker he had no knowledge of any current or future indictments. Schultz should have told him, "If there are any, I can't comment." The bigger question is, Why did Parker deny he talked to any prosecutors before Roberts's trial? I believe such an admission might support a charge of conspiracy to obstruct justice, and Parker wasn't dumb.

Before Goins ended the deposition, he got Deputy Chief Parker to once again deny he ever gave *Star Tribune* reporter David Chanen derogatory information about me. Finally Parker admitted he had never read Sgt. Zabel's report, but then again, it didn't matter. Deputy Chief Parker was happy with what he got from VOTF, according to Maj. Wagner. Parker couldn't care less about Zabel's report. His only concern seemed to be getting even with me for turning him and his friends in to the Justice Department.

In the summer of 2012, Capt. Wright was deposed. Wright said that Maj. Yates told him I had compromised an ATF wiretap and made an unauthorized disclosure, but the cover story that I made an unauthorized disclosure was shattered when Parker, with Yates sitting right next to him, admitted to me it was bogus. Nevertheless, Yates told that to Capt. Wright. Wright also said Officer Hardy was the one who went to Internal Affairs and claimed I violated the wiretap, which lends credence to the theory that Hardy was deeply involved in the cover story. Wright, true to form, was cocky from start to finish, but he gave up great information about Yates and Hardy. However, he denied ever supplying any reporters with negative information about me despite cell phone records indicating he may have.

In the fall of 2012, Officer Baker was deposed. Baker confirmed he had complained to Capt. Robinson about me and they discussed the MPD/ATF case in Faribault, which became the cover story, in early August 2007. Baker probably didn't realize it, but that admission seemed to put him squarely in the middle of the infamous cover story and the false claim that I made an unauthorized disclosure. Baker confirmed he told Capt. Robinson that I was obstructing the FBI public corruption case, but Robinson was not in the know or involved in the public corruption case at that point, so she had no clue what was going on. What Baker was really saying was that I was demanding the FBI and US attorneys follow the letter of the law, but Baker interpreted that for

Capt. Robinson as "obstructing justice." The man who was obstructing justice might have been Baker.

VOTF officers were telling a lot of stories, and in 2012, during his federal court deposition, Officer Lance Speer claimed he worked on the FBI public corruption case "half the time." Speer was adamant he spent "half the time" on the FBI public corruption case—50 percent of his time—but in his state court deposition in 2010, over two years earlier, Officer Speer told a completely different story. He said he spent only "three percent" of his time on the public corruption case. He went further and claimed he had "virtually no involvement." Officer Speer gave two completely different stories regarding his role in the public corruption investigation.

In 2010, when Officer Speer was deposed in state court, he knew that I was suing the MPD and that the truth would invariably come out about the public corruption case, so he did everything he could to distance himself from all the criminal misconduct surrounding that case. Speer, Hardy, Baker, Denton, and Evans all seemingly played a major role in instigating and misleading the FBI and US attorney's office when it first started. So over two years later, in a federal court deposition, Speer was now trying to turn everything around, but it was too late. The paper trail was well established. No matter how hard he tried, he couldn't turn 3 percent into 50 percent, and his "virtually no involvement" answer made it very clear.

CHAPTER 12
THE CONSPIRACY

IN THE FALL OF 2012, MAJ. OWENS WAS DEPOSED. HE CLAIMED THAT Sgt. Burt's March 2010 Internal Affairs complaint had been investigated over a "period of weeks," but he could not provide any proof or documents confirming any such investigation had occurred. Furthermore, Owens seemed evasive and vague. Nonetheless, he insisted Capt. Huffman had conducted the investigation. That didn't make any sense either, because captains seldom conduct investigations. And I made it clear to Goins and Ward that I thought Owens was not being truthful. Owens seemed to exaggerate his investigative career, and I did not trust him, so I pushed hard to have Owens brought back for a second deposition while I looked into his claim of an investigation over a "period of weeks."

Later in the day, my lawyers attempted to depose Officer Denton again, but he claimed he was available only for a few minutes. Mr. Goins said, "Fine; we will depose him for a few minutes and bring him back tomorrow." That was not what Denton wanted to hear, but he had backed himself into a corner and had no choice but to sit down. Denton looked totally freaked out when he came into the lawyer's conference room. He seemed nervous and scared. I could tell he wanted to get out of there as fast as possible. He knew by now that Goins and Ward were skilled lawyers. But in his short deposition, he still denied providing confidential, false, and negative information to reporters Lyden and Chanen about me.

A few days later, Officer Denton was once again on the hot seat in front of Goins and Ward. He didn't seem to like it one bit. Denton invoked the "I don't recall" and the "I don't remember" lines and similar words more than 340 times during his deposition as he dodged culpability for the media attacks. Denton testified that he believed FBI agent Turner and FBI agent Alinsky were the two agents who went to Deputy Chief Parker and requested my removal from VOTF. Denton didn't want to talk about anything he did, but he seemed to have no problem accusing other officers and FBI agents.

Goins and Ward sensed Denton might be ready to give up somebody or something, and they were right. Denton opened up the hatch and started carpet-bombing. He certainly wasn't an F16 fighter pilot with laser-guided missiles and precision. He was more like a wounded B-17 pilot chugging along to get back to base and just opening the hatch. At this point he was scared to death of Goins and his commanding voice and Ward's serious stare. He hoped that if he started carpet-bombing, they would ease up on him. They did a little, but they made sure he knew they were no fools. He was the private and they were the generals. That point was made very clear.

Most people involved in criminal misconduct seldom give up everything unless they have been given a deal from the government, and even then they still leave out bits of self-preservation. Denton still likely has a lot more to tell, but whatever he says in the future, it must be corroborated with additional facts and a polygraph in exchange for any potential leniency.

Nevertheless, Denton dropped several bombs in the fall of 2012, and in no particular order. Denton's goal that day seemed to be to give Goins and Ward enough to keep himself from a complete and total mental breakdown. His most alarming admission was when he **admitted that Sgt. Shaw shared details of my compelled June 2008 Internal Affairs statement with him, but he "could not recall" all the details. It didn't matter; even with that little bit of information, he seemingly admitted to taking part in a potential criminal conspiracy. Denton went further and testified there was direct communication between Stahl and the US DOJ IG. There was dead silence. My attorneys and**

I couldn't believe what he had just said. Denton had just testified there was communication between the US DOJ IG and assistant US attorney Stahl. Did the US DOJ IG tip off the feds in Minneapolis, or was it all an accident, as they claimed? Regardless, Denton's testimony clearly implied potential collusion between VOTF, Internal Affairs, the Minneapolis US attorney's office, and maybe even the US DOJ IG. I do not believe Denton was being completely honest when he said he could not recall all the details regarding what Shaw told him, but that seeming amnesia can easily be fixed with a federal grand jury and a special prosecutor.

No matter how you cut it, the link is there for potential collusion, conspiracy, and a whole lot more. Denton and Evans can possibly provide the framework for a RICO case. Make them talk and corroborate their statements with polygraphs, and it's game over. The house will fall.

The attorneys deposed Sergeant Matthew Bright the next day. Bright testified that he and other black police officers sued the MPD in 2007 for unjustly demoting and transferring black officers. Commanders removed Bright from the homicide unit for talking to the media about a case, but they did nothing to his white partner, who also apparently talked to the media. Ironically, I gave Internal Affairs evidence of white cops calling the media and making up false statements about me, but Parker and his friends never did a thing. Bright said a white Minneapolis police commander ridiculed Bright during a live radio talk show, and the Minneapolis Police Union tried to get the commander charged criminally, but a local county prosecutor declined charging. The Police Officers Federation of Minneapolis stood up for a black police sergeant who was being maligned by his white boss. It was the first of many attempts throughout this entire ordeal whereby the police union did their best to protect black officers who were being publicly and privately ridiculed by the white powers that be in Minneapolis. In no uncertain terms, the MPD and the City of Minneapolis seemingly did nothing to protect black cops from bad white cops. On the other hand, the police union fought hard for them and did their best to make sure their rights were not violated.

Deputy Chief Parker alleged during a civil deposition that Sgt. Bright was under criminal investigation per the VOTF public corruption case. During the same deposition, Parker also admitted he tipped off the police union on October 5, 2007, about the secret MPD/FBI public corruption investigation. Deputy Chief Parker assumed I would never get access to his deposition. So he boasted that he had compromised the public corruption case, all the while telling others in the department that it was I who compromised the FBI public corruption investigation. An assistant chief was blaming his lieutenant for the crime I believe he may have committed. It's not supposition or conjecture; he admitted to it in a sworn deposition.

The first time Sgt. Bright heard anything about the public corruption case was when Deputy Chief Parker falsely alleged that he was a target of the investigation. The fact of the matter is that on the night of Jackson's arrest, Jackson was adamant Matthew Bright was not involved. I made that clear to Deputy Chief Parker and everyone else. In time they would see that virtually everything Jackson said was either false or a gross exaggeration.

Matthew Bright confirmed that he and Jackson grew up in the same neighborhood and that it would be impossible for Jackson to confuse him and his brother, Mark, who was also a MPD officer. Matthew and Mark Bright were highly decorated MPD officers with years of exemplary service and were highly respected by their peers. Mark Bright is taller and has a lighter complexion, and people just do not confuse siblings they grew up with. Goins asked Matthew Bright whether Jackson could have reasonably confused him and his brother Mark, and he replied, "That's totally impossible." Matthew Bright said he had not seen Jackson in more than twenty years. Matthew and Mark Bright were tough, no-nonsense cops. They grew up in Minneapolis and came from a strong Christian family. Their mother and father were hardworking salt-of-the-earth people who were extremely proud of their sons. Matthew and Mark Bright served the City of Minneapolis with absolute distinction throughout their long and dedicated careers.

Sgt. Bright said the civil lawsuit involving him and four other African American offices was leaked to reporter David Chanen of the *Star Tribune*, and some believed Deputy Chief Parker was a likely source.

If that assumption is correct, it's another link between Deputy Chief Parker and Chanen.

The lawyers were doing a full-court press to get all the depositions done, and in the fall of 2012 they deposed Captain Kay Robinson. Robinson was in my chain of command as the commander of criminal investigations, and Robinson and I had a good working relationship. Robinson confirmed that Capt. Newton had accidentally exposed the public corruption case during a staff meeting in 2007. She also said that Deputy Chief Parker was my direct supervisor for the public corruption case. She and Newton were not privy to any of the investigation's details. It was between me and Deputy Chief Parker, per Parker's order.

Capt. Robinson testified that it was Officer Baker who told her that I compromised the ATF wiretap in Faribault, Minnesota, and made an unauthorized disclosure, which in turn became the infamous cover story. Robinson said Officers Evans, Speer, Hardy, and Denton corroborated Baker's claim about the false wiretap story. All five of them told her I made an unauthorized disclosure. These were the five cops who allegedly started the seeming corruption, and they—initially, at least—may have duped the FBI into believing it as well. If they didn't dupe the FBI, then the FBI was equally part of the potential conspiracy, because they had a legal and moral obligation to investigate the false claims.

I believe that when these five VOTF officers realized I would not cover up Jackson's false claims of rampant corruption among black police officers, they went into panic mode, fearing the loss of their overtime, take-home cars, and plum assignment. So they told the FBI supervisors multiple lies so they would go after me, but eventually somebody in the FBI allegedly told Shaw the cover story was bogus, but who was it? Or was Shaw lying about the mystery FBI agent? She claimed she didn't recall the agent's name. So either the FBI was duped and knew nothing about the cover story, or they were in on it and tried to stop a runaway train when they told Shaw it was unfounded.

Another possibility is that Shaw just made up everything about the phantom FBI agent and she was in on it from the beginning with Hardy, Speer, Baker, Denton,

and Evans. If the FBI was not part of the cover story, they have more than enough evidence to arrest Hardy, Speer, Baker, Denton, Evans, and Shaw for a number of potential crimes. If any of them told the FBI I violated the wiretap, I believe they should be arrested for lying to federal agents. Even if they didn't, I believe they most likely started this whole mess designed to secure their assignments and overtime and attack their peers for unaccountable overtime.

Robinson said the ATF never said anything to her about me until after Officer Baker told her the bogus unauthorized disclosure story. That is important because it leads credence to the theory that Baker and perhaps others recruited the ATF to help them fortify the bogus cover story. It's obvious Baker and other VOTF officers antagonized the ATF after, or just before, they planted the seed with Robinson. Seemingly it was all designed to get rid of me so they could keep the FBI public corruption case alive and guarantee themselves endless and unaccountable overtime, take-home cars, and a plum assignment.

Capt. Robinson further testified nobody ever told her that ATF agent Pedowski had apologized to me. And no one told her that assistant US attorney Folk authorized me to brief the Faribault police chief, his captain, and the Rice County sheriff about the Tre-Tre Crips wiretap case that extended into their jurisdiction before Folk provided them with all the details about the case. Robinson said my removal from VOTF took time. It was not a spur-of-the moment decision. This simple but honest statement that it was not a knee-jerk decision may play an important role in the future prosecution of the culpable parties. Robinson said it took time. Conspiracies require a certain level of time, collusion, and cooperation. Those innocent and truthful comments by Robinson provide credence to an alleged conspiracy. It wasn't a knee-jerk decision. There was planning, conniving, and calculated deceit.

Robinson further confirmed that she ordered me to reduce overtime because the City of Minneapolis was $6 million in the red and the only guaranteed city authorized overtime was for the public corruption case. Everything else was seriously reduced, scrutinized, or just plain prohibited.

Robinson confirmed that some VOTF officers had used up all of their 2007 federally authorized overtime of $15,600 by August, so their only chance at overtime would have to come from the public corruption case. If the public corruption case ended, so did the overtime. Officers' overtime generally can come only from their direct employer or a federal task force. Having a special or private overtime account drawing from government seizures without any checks and balances would certainly be an aberration, but apparently some VOTF officers were privy to this money train.

Robinson said Deputy Chief Parker told her that I was making it difficult for the FBI to move forward with the public corruption case, but he never told her that Jackson seemed to be a pathological liar, and he may have violated the conditions of his plea agreement. He left that part out.

Robinson said Parker was solely responsible for all demotions, promotions, suspensions, and terminations. Robinson said the main reason I was demoted was because I allegedly disclosed details of a wiretap to the Faribault Chief and Rice County Sheriff without authorization, but she quickly admitted to Goins that it would not have been a violation if it had been authorized. Goins then asked her whether anyone ever told her I was authorized, and she shockingly said, "No."

Robinson also said Sgt. Shaw never told any of the commanders that I was authorized to make the disclosure. Robinson said I was found guilty of making an unauthorized disclosure and she said she did not make the connection between Jackson's lies and the need to discredit me. She just believed them (Hardy, Speer, Baker, Denton, Evans, and Shaw) because I was outnumbered. Robinson said the missing $12,000 from the ICE fund should have warranted an Internal Affairs investigation, and if she had been in charge, there would have been one.

Capt. Robinson said the Internal Affairs director can take a case to any prosecuting attorney if an Internal Affairs case is criminal. Captain Jerry Hess did not. Robinson confirmed that officers are prohibited from using the tools and power of their office to benefit themselves financially. Robinson also confirmed that the Minnesota police and fire pension fund, known as Public Employees Retirement Association (PERA), bases police and fire pensions on how much police officers and firefighters make. The more money officers make, the bigger their pensions.

Robinson said Sgt. Burt's allegation that an MPD commander tried to divert $200,000 in FBI funds into the VOTF fund should have warranted an Internal Affairs investigation. Robinson further testified that nobody told her that Sgt. Zabel confirmed I never said anyone was being indicted, and Robinson embarrassingly admitted that the discipline panel, also known as the Laudermill Panel, found me guilty of making that statement even though it was false. Robinson said she had no idea my commander, Lucy Gerold, had asked me to give my opinion at the Third Precinct commander's meeting.

Capt. Robinson agreed it was inappropriate for Deputy Chief Parker to be the judge and jury of my April 2010 Internal Affairs complaint against him and his friends. Robinson confirmed I gave the Laudermill Panel evidence I had been in contact with the Department of Justice, but she had no idea whom I had turned in to the US Justice Department. Robinson said the Laudermill Panel affirmed the charges against me, and she never investigated anything. Robinson said she got her information and orders from Maj. Yates.

Finally, Goins asked Robinson whether she offered me a promotion to captain after I was removed from VOTF. She said, "Yes, Lieutenant Keefe has always been a good investigator." Like ATF agent Lawson, Robinson seems to have been used, and she didn't even know it. Capt. Robinson was intentionally excluded from the deception and deceit of the MPD command staff because they knew she would never help them frame me, so they fed her a pack of lies. Remember: the chain of command skipped her and Capt. Newton. Newton was skipped because of his big mouth, and Capt. Robinson was skipped because of her integrity. By the time the deposition was over, Robinson looked as if she wanted to give me a hug and apologize for all the hell I had been put through, but it just wasn't the appropriate time for an apology for not doing more. She seemed distraught over everything she had been told. She had seemingly been used by bad cops, but she set the record straight during her deposition.

CHAPTER 13
MISSISSIPPI BURNING

IN THE FALL OF 2012, DEPUTY CHIEF PARKER WAS DEPOSED FOR THE second time. During this deposition, Parker admitted his captain, Henry Newton, may have compromised the public corruption case accidentally during a commander's meeting in 2007. Parker denied destroying two letters of appreciation I received from a national company for work I was doing recovering stolen computers after Parker demoted me. I was seizing stolen computers left and right, and the company, LoJack, directly mailed Deputy Chief Parker two letters of appreciation for my outstanding work. What Parker didn't know was that they also mailed me copies. The letters were never placed in my personnel file. Parker conveniently denied he ever received the letters.

After I was demoted, I was assigned to the First Precinct Property Crimes Unit in downtown Minneapolis, and my lieutenant wasted no time giving me a heavy caseload. I felt I was being provoked, but I kept quiet because I felt that Parker and his boys were doing it on purpose. Besides, I enjoyed being busy, and I loved going after people who were making life miserable for everyone else. From October 5, 2009, until October 5, 2010, I was given ninety-three more cases than my peers, and I ended up filing twenty-seven felony criminal complaints while my peers had a total of eighteen. I should have been given annual performance evaluations, but I received none despite it being MPD policy.

On December 18, 2013, I sent an email to Caresa Meuwissen in the MPD personnel office, seeking my performance evaluations and letters of appreciation. I followed up with a phone call. The very next day, Meuwissen sent me an email informing me that I had no performance evaluations on file from 2009 through 2012.

Maj. Wagner was also deposed in the fall of 2012 for the second time. Wagner started out the deposition by telling Goins that a VOTF officer may have lied to assistant US attorney Hanson about a federal investigation. Wagner had no problem talking about other people, so attorney Goins proceeded to ask her about Sgt. Burt's Internal Affairs complaint that outlined how VOTF officers allegedly seized $50,000 from the Williams drug case and placed it in the VOTF overtime account rather than let the case proceed. Wagner reluctantly admitted it was not investigated. She then claimed that VOTF targeting criminals for money was not misconduct. Wagner also claimed an officer's alleged lies to assistant US attorney Hanson were simply a "management issue." My attorneys and I thought she was off her rocker. Wagner admitted the City of Minneapolis got stuck for the $12,000 missing from an ICE fund, and none of the VOTF officers were ever questioned or investigated. Goins had had enough of Wagner's nonsense, so he made her confirm she told Deputy Chief Parker that some VOTF officers had engaged in serious misconduct which was potentially criminal and warranted an internal investigation. But now, after she and Parker were exposed for not doing anything about it, it was time to try to rewrite the script and claim it was all just a "management issue." But it was futile. Wagner could not walk back her previous claims that serious VOTF misconduct warranted an investigation.

Wagner could not recover no matter how hard she tired, and eventually she reluctantly said her previous claims of VOTF misconduct could be subject to an Internal Affairs investigation. Goins stayed after Wagner and got her to admit she could launch an Internal Affairs investigation on her own. Wagner was also forced to admit that assistant US attorney Hanson told her a VOTF officer lied to her repeatedly, but yet she, a high-ranking police major, never opened an Internal Affairs investigation despite there being a very clear policy regarding officers lying. Wagner then tried to claim the VOTF officer's lies were not in official context. Listening to Wagner's nonsense was sickening and disgusting.

Every time Wagner tried to distance herself from her previous claims, Attorney Goins ripped her to pieces. Wagner reluctantly admitted that assistant US attorney Hanson told her she and other attorneys were given the okay to reject VOTF cases because some VOTF officers were untruthful with her and she did not trust them. Stop and think about that for a minute. The MPD would not police itself, and the FBI was seemingly afraid to do anything becasue they were apparently in bed together, so assistant US attorneys just took things into their own hands. Feeling the heat from Goins, Wagner seemed to decide it was time to throw Deputy Chief Parker under the bus. She proceeded to tell Goins that Parker told her that VOTF officers lying to assistant US attorney Hanson was not an official violation of department policy. Wow! Wagner went further and told Goins that Parker told her that within a couple of days after she and Capt. Reed told him about serious potential VOTF misconduct, Deputy Chief Parker said there would be no investigation. And just like that, the case was closed. No more questions. End of story. When Wagner said that, I immediately thought about the Neshoba County, Mississippi, Sheriff's Department in 1964 and the movie *Mississippi Burning*. (Hence the title of this book.)

The erratic demeanor and behavior of these officers under stress during their depositions made it appear they were unstable and could snap under pressure. On more than one occasion, Goins and Ward double-checked to make sure I was armed, and now I realized why. I felt we really were dealing with a band of unstable cops.

Maj. Wagner knew she was in the middle of a massive case of potential corruption, so after she finished throwing Parker under the bus, she turned to Major Jim Owens. She said she knew Owens was aware of Sgt. Burt's complaint, but she denied giving Owens a copy of Burt's report, even though she implied Owens had a copy. What was she really saying? Major Anna Wagner seemed to be throwing the Internal Affairs director, Captain Jerry Hess, under the bus for leaking Sgt. Burt's complaint to Maj. Owens. Goins wasn't about to ease up on Maj. Wagner just because she threw Capt. Hess and Maj. Owens under the bus for potential collusion. Goins kept after her and forced her to admit once again there was no Internal Affairs investigation for another department policy violation—damaging relationships with federal partners. Deputy Chief Parker and Sgt. Shaw charged me with allegedly violating this policy when I refused to be an FBI yes-man and cover up Jackson's lies, but when Parker's friends allegedly rolled dirty and crossed the FBI, the US attorney's office, and the DEA, it was a different story. They seemed to have impunity to do whatever they wanted.

Wagner further alleged that assistant US attorney Hanson had told him a VOTF officer withheld incriminating information from her about a confidential reliable informant (CRI), which could "potentially" justify an Internal Affairs investigation. Obviously, withholding information from an assistant US attorney you are working with on a case is serious business, and it clearly would justify a full-scale Internal Affairs investigation. That is how innocent people go to prison, and yet Wagner was claiming it could "potentially" justify an Internal Affairs investigation. A lying informant led VOTF into the wrong house and nearly got an innocent family and fellow officers killed. Not to mention that everything I was fighting about started out with a lying informant. Yet this arrogant police commander was acting as though it was no big deal.

Maj. Wagner was also forced to admit Hanson told her she suspected another VOTF officer was covering up evidence, and again Wagner said it could "potentially" justify an Internal Affairs investigation. Goins and Ward were furious with Major Anna Wagner's cocky, nonchalant attitude, and they kept after her until she admitted that nobody ever investigated the officers for allegedly withholding information from assistant US attorney Hanson. It seemed some officers were literally above the law.

Maj. Wagner tried to claim she didn't know whether I was found guilty for violating the MPD code of conduct regarding agency relationships, but she sat on the panel that sustained the charge. She was beyond weird. Wagner kept up with the nonsense and claimed she did not know assistant US attorney Folk had allowed me to make the initial wiretap disclosure to the Faribault police chief and the Rice County sheriff, and it's likely she didn't know because Shaw apparently withheld that evidence from all the commanders. But she did concede that if Folk had given me the okay, then no violation occurred.

Nevertheless, Wagner said she still believed I said indictments were pending, despite the sworn statements of Inspector Gerold and three other lieutenants who were at the meeting and had nothing to gain. Wagner couldn't help acting like a child. I found her to be naturally rude and abrasive. I thought nobody liked her. She was being humiliated and exposed for her own alleged misconduct, and like a spoiled little brat, she just could not take responsibility. Wagner said she agreed Sgt. Zabel was a good investigator, but she chose not to believe him or anyone else who backed me up. Wagner's ego prohibited her from accepting the results of Zabel's investigation because she was the officer who filed the bogus complaint against me after Sgt. Gemma Shaw sold her the ridiculous story about sealed indictments and officers being indicted. Shaw made her look like an idiot, and she just couldn't handle it.

Wagner was worn down, and so was everyone else. Listening to somebody like Wagner repeatedly play games was exhausting and frustrating. But fortunately, without even realizing it, Wagner threw Parker under the bus. Wagner said Deputy Chief Parker told her that Sheriff Stanek told him that I said there were "sealed indictments." This was a big deal because it never happened. On the contrary, Sheriff Stanek told Sgt. Zabel the "sealed indictments" story was not true. So Deputy Chief Parker seemed to have totally made that story up. Moreover, Zabel documented it in his report that Stanek confirmed I never said that. Remember that Parker suspended me on the eve of Roberts's trial because he claimed I was being "disruptive" and spreading rumors about officers being "indicted." The evidence clearly points to Parker and his allies spreading rumors and being disruptive, not me.

Wagner finished off her deposition with one last seeming lie. She claimed she could not remember whether she told Capt. Hess not to give me a Garrity warning. Wagner had already admitted she had in her previous deposition. Maj. Wagner's last flip-flop made it very clear she likely knew what she had done may have been criminal. She was in the middle of a massive case of criminal misconduct, and she didn't know which way to turn.

Maj. Wagner never filed any complaints against VOTF officers, despite what she was told by FBI agent O'Shea and assistant US attorney Hanson. Something was clearly wrong within the command structure of the MPD. Good cops just kept quiet for fear of being persecuted. They had nobody they could turn to or trust—not even the FBI. The powers that be had destroyed the police department. Internal Affairs was a joke, and the police union warned officers to be careful.

A few weeks later, Sgt. Andersen was deposed. Andersen said Sgt. Burt had a very good reputation and VOTF was out of control. He said the narcotics unit was just as successful as VOTF, but with virtually no overtime. The narcotics unit also seized more money. Andersen said VOTF operated with impunity, and it was well known they were untouchable. In fact, Andersen said Detective Jim Ryan told him he was embarrassed by how obvious it was that they were untouchable. Andersen said the MPD narcotics unit's commander, Capt. Huffman, was a higher-ranking captain than Kirby, but whenever VOTF officers wanted anything, Kirby would just go over Huffman's head to get their way.

Sgt. Andersen said everyone knows you always go after the dope for a stronger case, not the money, as Capt. Kirby did in the Williams case when she seized $50,000 for the VOTF overtime account. Andersen said the narcotics unit had between $250,000 and $260,000 in its seizure fund when it was disbanded and taken over by VOTF. According to Andersen, it was a very successful unit, but VOTF took over everything. Sgt. Andersen said lying about overtime is theft, and he agreed some VOTF officers had bad reputations. He noted that VOTF allowed an officer to stay in the unit despite being written up for serious misconduct.

Andersen said cops feared being transferred if they turned in VOTF officers because they were untouchable. Sgt. Andersen said he also feared retaliation because some VOTF officers were protected by Deputy Chief Parker.

Andersen said VOTF officer Mike Doran[real name?] told him they had to cover for Parker's friends or they would be removed from VOTF. He also said he heard VOTF officers celebrating over a wiretap they got approved. The officers were boasting because it meant more money on their pensions via the wiretap. Andersen, like Burt, was so fearful of retaliation that he consulted with police union attorneys before he gave his deposition. Sgt. Andersen said FBI agent O'Shea was honest and ethical and would not spread rumors or make unfounded statements. She was a top-notch FBI agent according to Andersen, and he said she worked a lot of cases from the ground up, but Officer Hardy degraded her as "just an administrator." Andersen said the MPD narcotics unit had the same stats as VOTF or better, with just a tenth of the overtime.

Andersen said VOTF did wiretaps for overtime instead of focusing on major players. He said the Williams case could have been charged without a wiretap, and when it was over, no major players were ever charged. It was a flop, but VOTF got $50,000 for overtime. Andersen confirmed that lying to a federal prosecutor was certainly grounds for an Internal Affairs investigation. He said some VOTF officers' overtime cannot be justified. Andersen also said Officer Mark Bright was a first-rate officer and had just recently been recommended for a Medal of Valor. He was the 1st Precinct Officer of the Year in 2012. He added that Matthew Bright was also a respected officer.

A few days later, in September of 2012, Minneapolis Police Department accountant Lilly Theis was deposed. Theis confirmed she sent an email to Capt. Robinson and me on August 16, 2007, advising us that some VOTF officers had maxed out their 2007 federal overtime allotments of $15,600, so the only overtime they could get for the rest of the year was city overtime. The city had ordered an end to all discretionary overtime because the city was $6 million in the red, so the only overtime available for VOTF officers was the public corruption case. If it had been shut down, that would have been the end to their overtime for the rest of the year. The loss of this overtime sent some of them into a tail spin.

Theis told Goins that Capt. Kirby tried to funnel the $50,000 seized from the Wayne Williams case in Chicago into the VOTF fund but that she stopped it because it was a DEA/MPD case. DEA forfeiture funds were not allowed into the MPD/FBI fund. Sgt. Burt had warned Lilly Theis that Kirby would try to do this, and sure enough, she did. Kirby was upset, so she called for a meeting with Maj. Owens and Theis to try to make her change her mind, but Theis stood her ground, and Kirby was denied the money. Theis was an honest and dedicated employee and she corroborated Burt's complaint.

Shortly thereafter, the City of Minneapolis received approximately $299,000 from a Department of Justice forfeiture certificate for a Chicago house that was seized and sold. All of that money, allegedly from the DEA case, somehow ended up in the MPD/FBI VOTF overtime fund, and not the DEA/MPD fund. How in the world did a small group of Minneapolis cops pull nearly $300,000 away from seized property in Chicago?

Theis said it was from a DOJ forfeiture certificate, but was it a "legitimate certificate" signed by all the appropriate parties? Was the DEA ever made aware of this? Did the DEA get any money from the seizure? Did the City of Chicago ever get any money? Needless to say, I do not believe the MPD under Deputy Chief Parker ever investigated anything involving Kirby and VOTF. A follow-up investigation of Burt's March 2010 Internal Affairs complaint would have provided the answers to all of these questions.

Theis said Capt. Kirby allegedly used seized funds to pay for the lease on her Chevy Tahoe, which amounted to somewhere between $600 and $700 a month. Theis also told Goins that VOTF officers had total access to ICE funds, and whenever they needed more money from ICE, they simply filled out a form and ICE sent the money. $12,000 was removed from an ICE agent's account when he was out of town, but again, there were no Internal Affairs investigations despite Sgt. Burt's detailed reports to Internal Affairs in 2010 regarding the missing $12,000.

On November 2, 2012, I sent B. Todd Jones, the US attorney for the State of Minnesota, a forty-six-page document detailing VOTF corruption. Jones never responded. What did Mr. Jones do with that forty-six-page report? Robert Mueller was the Director of the FBI in 2012.

CHAPTER 14
THE US DISTRICT COURT OF MINNESOTA

In a summary judgment, a plaintiff's attorneys and the defendant's attorneys briefly argue their case before a judge, and a judge then decides whether the case is worthy of trial. If the plaintiff loses, the case is dismissed unless the plaintiff appeals to a higher court. In this case, the higher court was the Eighth Circuit Court of Appeals, the most conservative court in the American federal judicial system.

On March 8, 2013, **lead** assistant city attorney David Nelson stood in front of US District Court judge David Doty and presented the city's case. Nelson told Judge Doty the MPD had conducted a **"robust investigation"** that was **"incredibly full"** as a result of two Internal Affairs cases. He claimed the MPD had conducted a **"good faith"** investigation and that the department had **"honestly believed"** the **"extensive investigation"** was proper. He went on to tell Judge Doty that the investigation was **"so full"** and **"incredibly full**," and he denied any retaliation. Nelson used the term **"extensively"** to describe Shaw's investigation, and he summed it up with the words **"honest belief"** and he also claimed there was no **"pretext."** Nelson said, "There is no evidence that the basis of the employment decision has no basis, in fact, because of the robust investigation."

In reality, I believed the entire investigation was nothing but pretext, starting with the bogus cover story that was used as a tool to remove me from VOTF so that the MPD, FBI, and US attorney's office could cover up Jackson's apparent lies and go after black cops.

Nelson told Judge Doty the case was "so full" and I "was—he was treated with care. He was given a "full investigation." My belief was that a so-called "full investigation" would have resulted in Officer Hardy's suspension and termination, and Shaw's as well for covering his tracks. Nelson had dug such a deep hole it didn't matter, and there was no turning back now. Nelson also told Judge Doty, "He [I] told a Minneapolis Internal Affairs investigator that other employees of the department were being indicted." In my mind, Nelson should have known that Sgt. Zabel had confirmed that Shaw made this up. Nelson also told Judge Doty that the MPD had honestly believed that their decisions were made in good faith.

Nelson told Doty there was no retaliation. I believed there was relentless retaliation. Nelson claimed that all my reports were the "same stuff." On the contrary, my complaints were about racism, overtime abuse, MPD misconduct, FBI misconduct, US attorney misconduct, and several other violations, including pretext and covering up exculpatory evidence. In my opinion, all these issues were not even close to being the "same stuff."

Nelson went further and said the discipline panel couldn't remember what they were told, but everyone on the panel testified that the Internal Affairs investigator had withheld crucial exculpatory evidence. In no uncertain terms, all four commanders matter-of-factly testified in their depositions that Shaw withheld evidence from them that would have exonerated me.

In my opinion, virtually nothing Nelson said during the summary judgment was true.

Nelson's claims paid off, and I lost the summary judgment. Attorneys Goins and Ward immediately appealed to the Eighth Circuit Court of Appeals.

On August 20, 2013 I sent the new internal affairs commander, Lt. Sean Burke, a detailed letter regarding the misconduct of Shaw and VOTF officers and I told him I believed I was being framed by Shaw. A few weeks later I had a private meeting with Burke, and Deputy Chief Craig Lambert, and I made it very clear I believed Shaw and others had committed a number of crimes. Burke was receptive and understandably alarmed, but Lambert was aloof and apathetic so a few weeks later I sent Lambert a very detailed follow up letter on December 13, 2013 summarizing our meeting and the alleged corruption I outlined and the evidence I gave him. Lambert responded by sending me a letter on January 6, 2014 claiming all my concerns about internal corruption had already been "reviewed." Not investigated, but "reviewed." A term commonly used when law enforcement officers are trying to dodge responsibility, and/or criminal culpability. I wasn't the least bit surprised. I knew Lambert wouldn't do anything. He wasn't fooling me one bit. I gave Deputy Chief Lambert everything I could including a copy of my forty-six page summary of the corruption which I sent to Minnesota US Attorney B. Todd Jones in 2012. I believe Lambert had more than enough evidence to take down multiple officers, agents, and attorneys, and all he had to do was launch a full scale internal and external investigation, but he did none of the above. He failed the integrity test just like Wagner and Parker did in 2010. I believe Lambert's failure to act and his disingenuous letter put him squarely in the middle of the corruption with Parker, Yates, and Wagner.

On January 4, 2014, I sent newly elected mayor Betsy Hodges a thirteen-page summary of alleged VOTF and MPD corruption. This was the first of three letters. The second (seven pages) was sent on January 13, 2014, and the third (six pages) was sent on February 6, 2014. After all three were sent to Hodges via interoffice mail, I hand-delivered all three as well. Mayor Hodges was personally standing in her office when I delivered one of the three with MPD Sgt. Helmer as a witness.

On February 10, 2014, at 9:55 a.m., after I sent Mayor Betsy Hodges those detailed letters regarding alleged corruption and a fourth letter explaining how I believe Capt. Reed had turned a blind eye to the alleged corruption, Mayor Hodges sent out a citywide email regarding a recent fire department investigation of a former fire chief. Hodges started out by saying how sorry she was that city employees had to suffer through bullying, retribution, and retaliation. She thanked those employees who came forward and cooperated in the investigation and noted that it was because of "[their] courageous actions in bringing forward the complaints that the City was able to conduct its investigation." Hodges went on to say there had been an "extremely thorough investigation" and that what the city learned through the process was "very troubling."

Hodges continued: "We hold our city leaders to the highest standards. It is clear from the investigation that our expectations for a department head were not met here. As the Mayor of this City, I want to reassure all employees that we are 100% committed to providing a respectful, positive work environment for everyone. Moreover, all employees must feel safe that they can come forward with concerns and issues without fear of retaliation. This is the policy of this City and that policy will be enforced."

Hodges continued, "As set out in the City's Anti-Discrimination, Harassment, and Retaliation policy, City leaders are to be held to the very highest standards of conduct. That is not only my expectation, but my requirement for all department heads and leaders. You are entitled to no less." I suspected it was all political hogwash, and in due time Hodges confirmed it.

In the spring of 2014, my lawyers deposed Maj. Owens for the second time. I had been waiting for this for a long time. Owens had told me and my attorneys during his first deposition that Capt. Huffman conducted a thorough investigation of Sgt. Burt's March 2010 Internal Affairs complaint over a "period of weeks," but I was immediately suspicious because Huffman was a captain and was not assigned to Internal Affairs. Furthermore, Owens used the "I don't recall" and "I believe" lines one too many times. I was convinced he was not telling the truth about the so-called "investigation," so Goins and Ward called Owens back for a second deposition. Was Owens lying to cover the tracks of his friends in VOTF? He invoked the "I don't recall" line more than sixty times and the "I believe" line more than sixty times, and his answers were suspicious. I wasn't buying any of it.

Maj. Owens went even further this time and again claimed that Capt.

Huffman had done an "investigation." Owens said, "It was reviewed 'point by point' by Capt. Huffman who presented a briefing of her investigation to myself and Deputy Chief Parker." Albert Goins wasted no time jumping all over Owens after that line of garbage. Owens's ego was getting the best of him, and he was about to bury himself.

> GOINS: What did she base her point-by-point briefing on?
> OWENS: The discussions she had with people and an explanation of how supervisors operated the unit.
> GOINS: This discussion she had with people—what does that mean, sir?
> OWENS: Well, she talked to individuals, I believe, within the unit and with federal partners to include the FBI agents who were working with Safe Streets Task Force, a.k.a. VOTF, and, I believe, ATF agents as well.
> GOINS: Can you name any?
> OWENS: No.
> GOINS: Did she take any Garrity statements?
> OWENS: No.
> GOINS: Do you know the names of federal partners she talked to?
> OWENS: No.

Goins had all he needed. Damon Ward casually looked over at me and smiled as soon as Owens said, "I believe." It was a red flag, big time. Owens never gave up any names. If there had been an investigation, Owens would have dropped names left and right. Attorneys Goins and Ward had Owens backed into a corner. All they had to do now was depose Capt. Huffman if the court would allow it. The city was objecting to all the depositions, so perhaps Owens thought he would be the last cop to be deposed, but he was wrong.

By the end of Owens's deposition, he had sworn under oath as a Minneapolis police major that Capt. Huffman had done a thorough and extensive "point-by-point" investigation of Sgt. Burt's detailed 2010 Internal Affairs complaint over "a period of weeks." Owens was very clear, and there was no confusion. He had sworn under oath there had been a legitimate police investigation.

Weeks later, the court allowed my lawyers to depose Capt. Huffman, and she wasted no time setting the record straight. In fact, she couldn't wait to set the record straight. Without hesitation, and in no uncertain terms, she told the attorneys and I that she never conducted any such investigation of anyone in VOTF and that she never even had the resources or authority to do such an investigation because she was not assigned to Internal Affairs. Huffman flat-out denied she ever did a "point-by-point" investigation of anything, let alone over a "period of weeks." Huffman said Sgt. Burt's Internal Affairs complaint was shut down within a matter of a few days, somewhere between three days and a week. End of story. Huffman smashed Owens's investigation story into a million pieces within a matter of minutes. The look on her face was incredulous when Goins asked her questions, and she seemed irritated that anyone would have the audacity to make such a preposterous claim.

It was a bad day for the MPD, because Capt. Huffman's testimony contradicted that of Maj. Owens. Huffman was adamant and spoke with confidence. She correctly noted that such an investigation would have generated a detailed paper trail, and she had no such documents, much less the authority to carry out such an investigation. Owens not just once, but twice, testified under oath about an investigation that had, according to Huffman, never occurred.

On May 21, 2014, Mayor Betsy Hodges was deposed for the first time. The deposition was without a doubt the weirdest and most bizarre of the federal and state court depositions. Like the others, it seemed to me to be full of game-playing.

The deposition started out with attorney Goins asking how long she had been on the city council prior to being elected mayor. She said she didn't know. Right there and then, the attorneys and I knew she was going to be a problem. Goins then asked her for her work address at city hall, and she said she didn't know her office or room number. Goins then asked her whether she knew that in the City of Minneapolis the chief of police gets to be the judge and jury of any complaints filed against him or her. Hodges said she had no idea. It was time to play dingbat. She started out being rude and weird, but the minute Goins hinted at criminal culpability she played dingbat. She wasn't stupid. She knew what she was doing.

Goins then asked her what she would do if anyone complained to her about the chief, and she said she would contact the city attorney. Goins asked her about documents I personally gave her on January 4, 2014, and she said she gave the documents to the city attorney. She claimed she never read any of the documents, so Goins asked her why this was. Hodges replied, "Because I didn't want to contaminate my memory of having received or not received the letter." The mayor of a major American city just said what? Goins persisted, and she said, "I didn't want to read the letter because I hadn't read the letter when it arrived." What kind of game was this woman playing? Goins then asked her whether she read her emails, and she said, "Sometimes." Translation? She seemed to be saying she never read any of my emails.

So here in the opening minutes of the deposition, the mayor of Minneapolis was dodging questions left and right, seemingly acting like a child, and passing the buck to the city attorney's office. And nobody in the city attorney's office ever turned my documents over to an outside law enforcement agency, despite my outline of multiple cases and examples of potential criminal misconduct. What kind of a public institution was this?

Hodges claimed she never read the thirteen-page document I handed to her secretary while she was standing directly in front of me and said hello. After Hodges told Goins she never read the document, Goins put the deposition on hold while she read it. After she read it, he asked her whether she was familiar with any of the allegations, and she said, "I don't know." It was unbelievable. She was the mayor of Minneapolis. She seemed to be evasive under the color of law because I believe she had potential criminal culpability for failing to act and hold potentially corrupt officers accountable. She seemed to be running scared but managed to be cocky and rude all the way.

Goins switched gears and asked Hodges how many years she had been on the city council. She quickly replied, "Eight," even though just a few minutes earlier she had said she didn't know. Hodges then proudly proclaimed she didn't vote for the reappointment of Chief Dolan because of his poor performance with racial issues and police accountability. But when I, with another sworn officer, Sgt. Helmer, as my witness, handed Hodges multiple documents outlining police corruption, she seems to have done nothing about it other than passing it to the city attorney.

Goins asked her whether she ever saw my 2010 Internal Affairs complaint. "Not that I recall," she answered. Goins then asked her whether she had ever seen Sgt. Burt's 2010 Internal Affairs complaint. Hodges answered, "Not that I recall." Goins outlined several issues, and all she could say was, "Not that I recall," "I believe," and every other possible way she could think of to avoid taking ownership or responsibility for being the mayor in charge of a city with a massive case of potential police corruption fueled by racial antipathy and money. After the deposition, my lawyers and I just shook our heads. Mayor Hodges was beyond weird, but perhaps she was smart enough to avoid any potential future criminal charges. The police department had been boiling in what I believed was corruption for several years, and Hodges was apparently too scared to touch it.

After Mayor Hodges's deposition, on June 10, 2014, I sent the acting US attorney for Minnesota, Andy Luger, a detailed two-page letter exposing the corruption, along with several attachments of previous letters to the DOJ seeking an investigation. Luger never responded. What did Mr. Luger do with my letter and supplemental reports? James Comey was the Director of the FBI in 2014.

On July 2, Mayor Hodges was deposed for the second time.

This time she played the attorney-client privilege game after attorney Goins asked her what she had done about corruption in the department since her previous deposition, when she allegedly read my complaint for the first time. Hodges grudgingly claimed she had been told everything had already been investigated, so she had done basically nothing. Whoever told her that was obviously lying, and she seemed to accept it.

Hodges seemed to be relentlessly evasive and refused to own

anything. She did admit a racial slur would warrant an Internal Affairs investigation, but short of that, not much else. It was like pulling teeth getting her to admit that $12,000 missing from an ICE account warranted an internal investigation. Hodges invoked the "I don't know" line more than fifty times, and she repeatedly tried to avoid answering Goins's questions. It was a pathetic display of leadership and accountability.

Why didn't she do anything? Was she misled by the city attorney, or was it the FBI? Or was she worried about losing a lawsuit or possibly even being criminally charged herself? Regardless, she had plenty of time to do something, but she did absolutely nothing.

Hodges's last deposition started out with assistant City attorney Nelson being rude, as usual, and this time attorney Damon Ward put him in his place. Ward set him straight in two minutes flat, but true to form, he continued to fight, apparently trying to impress the mayor. Nelson was no match for Ward either. Mr. Ward was an engineer before switching occupations and becoming a lawyer. Like Goins, he was a brilliant man and was beyond reproach.

It was the weirdest thing ever. To me, Hodges seemed to act like a spoiled little schoolgirl rather than the mayor of Minneapolis. I felt she pretended to know nothing. She was arrogant, cocky, and rude. I couldn't believe what I was seeing and hearing. Her answers were beyond bizarre. I wasn't sure whether she was intimidated by Goins and Ward or whether she just wanted to play games. I had no doubt the city attorneys told her Goins and Ward were brilliant men, and maybe that had her a bit concerned. Hodges claimed to have never read any of my letters. She also denied reading the letters after they were given to her before her deposition. She was beyond weird. She was literally creepy.

CHAPTER 15
THE EIGHTH CIRCUIT COURT OF APPEALS

On October 7, 2014, Albert Goins and Damon Ward argued my case before a three-judge panel of the Eighth Circuit Court of Appeals in St. Paul, Minnesota. The city sent attorney David Nelson and his co-counsel attorney Lee Johnson, as well as another attorney, Katie Olson.

There was only one way the city could win the case, and that was to repeat the fairy tales they told Judge Doty. That is exactly what they did, and they went further this time, knowing Capt. Huffman had confirmed that one of the highest-ranking members of the MPD, Maj. Owens, had provided sworn statements that did not seem to conform to the truth regarding the so-called investigation of Sgt. Burt's complaint of internal corruption. Owens's testimony was just a speck in the big picture, but it was extremely important because it was an attempt to discredit Burt's complaint, which corroborated my complaint. The big question is, why did he do it? Did someone ask him to do it? If so, who?

The hearing started out with Albert Goins speaking first, but he was rudely interrupted several times by a judge who, it seemed to me, already had his mind made up. When it was time for Nelson to speak, he wasn't interrupted, and he seemingly took everything to another level.

Nelson told the court that **"Keefe falsely reported misconduct by another officer that he knew wasn't true."** This did not conform to the truth. Yes, I filed a complaint with Internal Affairs about another officer, and my complaint was corroborated by Sergeant Andersen. Other officers testified they never heard the misconduct, but Andersen provided graphic testimony in his sworn deposition with an assistant city attorney at his side.

It's hard to tell what fairy tale Nelson was talking about when he claimed, "Keefe falsely reported misconduct by another officer that he knew wasn't true." It's possible he was making a reference to an officer I removed from the task force for vulgar and sexist remarks in front of a young female FBI agent. An FBI supervisor backed me up and referred to this officer as a "bully." In my summary of the officer's misconduct, I had a couple irrelevant details wrong, according to Denton and Evans, but the officer's transfer out of VOTF was clearly justified. Perhaps Nelson was trying to make a mountain out of this anthill to justify his statements that did not conform to the truth.

Nelson told the court that command officers "couldn't **remember**" the evidence they were provided, but that felt misleading. All four commanders testified Shaw never told them the "cover story" was a ruse. All four of them testified the Internal Affairs investigator withheld evidence from them. Their memories were very clear.

Nelson told the court I was a "**huge problem.**" He further claimed "**he made this unauthorized disclosure.**" Nelson was sitting right next to Shaw when she said the FBI told her I never made an unauthorized disclosure. Nelson was also aware that retired MN BCA Agent Jim Hessell confirmed I never made any unauthorized disclosure, but nevertheless Nelson relayed it to the court. In short, Nelson told the court the infamous cover story was legitimate.

Nelson told the court I was guilty of "**repeated severe employment misconduct**" and was not a "team player." It's true I would not help corrupt officers, agents, and attorneys cover up evidence, but I was never guilty of any "severe employment misconduct." In fact, despite it all, I still outperformed all my peers, year in and year out.

Nelson told the court the MPD spent an "**enormous amount of time and patience**" on the case. In my mind, an enormous amount of time and patience would have exposed the alleged corruption.

Nelson told the court there was no pretext for racism and there was "**so much evidence supporting his demotion.**" Nelson likely knew Sgt. Burt's Internal Affairs case noted racism, and he also likely knew that four command officers had testified that if they had known the cover story was a ruse, **I would never have been demoted.**

Nelson told the court there was "**some evidence he leaked evidence.**" Leaked what? To whom? Nelson was sitting right next to Shaw when she testified that the FBI told her I never made an unauthorized disclosure. Shaw clearly testified that the FBI said, "Lt. Keefe was not going to be accused of that misconduct." Furthermore, a retired MN BCA agent also confirmed I never leaked anything or miscarried in any way, but Nelson told the court I did.

I believe Nelson, the lead attorney for the city of Minneapolis assigned to this case from start to finish, who sat in on several depositions and argued the case, should be compelled to testify before a federal grand jury under the direction of a special prosecutor and ordered to back up his claims.

During the hearing, one of the judges asked Nelson whether any of it was a ruse, and Nelson said the record supports Judge Doty's decision. He never answered the judge's question. He changed the subject. That judge sensed something was amiss, but Nelson outsmarted him and redirected everything back to Judge Doty, and the judge backed off. Another judge asked Nelson whether I ever did anything to impede the FBI investigation, and Nelson replied, "I guess we will never know if he shared information." The record is clear that I never shared any information, tipped anyone off, or made an unauthorized disclosure, but Nelson left them hanging anyway, and by doing so, he implied I did.

Finally, a judge can be heard on the tape saying, "It seemed to be a fair amount of process." Nothing could have been further from the truth.

Minnesota statute 481.07, Penalties for Deceit or Collusion, was designed for attorneys who mislead in court. The statute states, "An attorney who, with intent to deceive a court or a party to an action or judicial proceeding, is guilty of or consents to any deceit or collusion, shall be guilty of a misdemeanor, and, in addition to the punishment prescribed therefor, the attorney shall be liable to the party injured in trebel damages."

On May 11, 2105, the Eighth Circuit Court of Appeals upheld Judge Doty's decision, and I lost the case. Within hours of losing his case, I swung back at the powers that be in Minneapolis. They had pulled off an incredible feat, but I wasn't about to give up. They were celebrating, but I let them know it wasn't over.

I sent an email to Mayor Hodges, the entire city council, and the Minneapolis police union. I made it clear it wasn't over. I called for a federal grand jury investigation. Calling for a federal grand jury criminal probe undoubtedly sent chills down the backs of Nelson, Parker, Reed, and everyone else who I thought was helping them keep a lid on this massive case of seemingly criminal misconduct. I asked the mayor and the city council for their support, but they all ran and hid. Two council members, Cam Gordon and Lisa Bender, did reply to my email, but at the end of the day, they did nothing. If there is an honorable city council member left in the city of Minneapolis, he or she should turn over every email he or she ever received from city attorneys regarding my fight for justice.

So why didn't the mayor and city council back me up and support a full-scale criminal investigation? The current mayor, Jacob Frey, who was a council member in 2015, received my email just like every other council member. He also did nothing. Why? Who was the decision-maker? Was it the city attorney? Was it about money? The case would have undoubtedly been a multimillion-dollar payout. Was it hate? Were the powers that be in Minneapolis so full of hatred for police officers in general that they were willing to do anything to frame some cops? Or did the FBI lie and claim they were already on the case? None of it made any sense.

Was the FBI so embarrassed that they helped start this whole mess after being duped by low-level cops who wanted unlimited overtime and take home-cars that they just looked the other way? Clearly the FBI knew by now they had gotten into bed with the wrong team—a rogue group of spoiled cops who were protected by incompetent and unethical police commanders—commanders who conspired with VOTF officers to use the media and their city cell phones to destroy my reputation and career on the eve of Roberts' trial, and commanders who shut down Internal Affairs cases that targeted them and their friends and made sure the department never had a conflict-of-interest policy that would mandate a neutral, outside agency investigation of internal corruption. Minneapolis was boiling with corruption, and there was plenty of blame to go around.

Today those emails are the city council's worst nightmare. They have blamed the police and the police union for everything, but I believe it was the city council and mayor who turned a blind eye to alleged corruption and allowed the pot to boil. They failed the citizens of Minneapolis. They allowed a rogue group of undisciplined, spoiled brat cops who never paid their dues and never worked the streets as police officers for more than two years to run wild, and they covered the tracks of commanders who should have been demoted and fired.

The MPD had no time or place for good cops. Veteran cops who had worked the street for years wouldn't even get a thank-you when they retired, but if one was part of the "in crowd," it didn't matter how many cases you mishandled or how much overtime you stole; you were a hero. The culture of the MPD was a ticking time bomb, and the FBI seemingly turned a blind eye to all of it.

The FBI could get to the bottom of all this in no time. There are several different ways they could go about it, but they know that no matter what route they take, it all comes back to those two high-ranking agents calling on Deputy Chief Parker to remove me from my command. Many attorneys would argue that was a potential criminal act under the color of law, so is that why the FBI won't take down the MPD?

According to several attorneys, those two FBI agents and their superior agents and assistant US attorneys who authorized everything might have the potential for significant criminal culpability, and maybe that is why the FBI has buried its head in the sand for so many years. I believe that the FBI decision to ask Deputy Chief Parker to remove me from my command possibly came from, at the very least, the Minneapolis FBI SSA, Kevin Irving, but it's more likely it came from the

Minneapolis FBI SAC or higher-ups in Washington, DC. When I was the commander of VOTF, I saw the FBI go up the chain of command for simple decisions, and for major decisions they routinely went all the way out to Washington, so I have no doubt the FBI orders came from very senior command agents and attorneys.

After notifying the elected officials in the City of Minneapolis, I kept up the pressure and contacted the chairman of the US Senate Judiciary Committee, Sen. Charles Grassley, on September 3, 2015.

My letter to Grassley was ten pages long. Within a few weeks, Sen. Grassley's staff and I were having good telephone conversations, and I could tell someone was finally doing his job. I understood it was at times a very confusing case to follow, so it naturally took Grassley's lawyer and staff several weeks to get a handle on everything. Furthermore, the bad cops, agents, and attorneys had run so much interference and told so many lies and manufactured so much phony evidence that it was a tangled web that was difficult to figure out. Nevertheless, Grassley's attorney, Jay Lim, and his staff figured it out.

Meanwhile, the city of Minneapolis was working on more retaliation to try to keep me quiet. On October 1, 2015, the City of Minneapolis, per the city attorney's office, sent me a letter advising me they had placed me on a Brady list—a list for officers who have been found to have used excessive force or engaged in other misconduct. So if I testified in any court proceedings, a defense lawyer could claim that I had been found guilty of filing a false report about a fellow officer and falsely claimed fellow officers were being indicted, and that I compromised a federal wiretap by tipping off a sheriff and a police chief about a federal investigation in their community without proper authorization. Basically, these were the nuts and bolts of all their lies and corruption.

Minneapolis was acting way outside the boundaries of any established protocol, but few knew it. That would all change in due time. The City of Minneapolis had openly and arrogantly retaliated. Apparently they thought it was now okay to hang their hat on Sgt. Shaw's allegedly corrupt investigation. They disregarded Sgt. Zabel's case and all the evidence alleging Shaw had repeatedly violated Internal

Affairs policy and, most importantly, how she allegedly covered VOTF officers' tracks and seemingly framed me, not to mention how she seems to have conspired with the feds and used the Internal Affairs office to determine whether I had a tape of Jackson lying.

The city's actions only motivated me to fight back more, and on November 9, I reached out to Minneapolis Human Resources and asked investigator Sandy Stokes to conduct an investigation of the Internal Affairs cases Shaw and her supervisors had used to allegedly frame me. Stokes told me she would most likely be able to get my case farmed out to an outside law firm, so I agreed to meet with her and provide her with confidential information. Finally, after all this, an outside agency would be involved.

On November 10, I sent Stokes an email with twelve investigative attachments, including the forty-six-page memo to Minnesota US Attorney B. Todd Jones and a thirteen-page letter outlining the corruption. I gave her pretty much everything. In no uncertain terms, she had enough evidence to fire several officers and submit criminal charges.

On November 29, I sent Stokes an additional nine-page letter to help her with her "investigation."

On December 7, Stokes sent me a letter stating that the information I sent to the investigative unit of the Employee Services Division in Human Resources had been "reviewed" (this being the second time they used that term) and that she had concluded that even if the allegations were found to have merit, they would not constitute a violation of the City's antidiscrimination, harassment, and retaliation policy. Consequently, no further "investigation" would be conducted by that office. This was literally unbelievable. Thirty-two days after I called her, and without her ever taking a statement from me or anyone else, her office slammed the door shut on a ton of alleged criminal misconduct. Who had allowed her to do something so egregious? I thought had to be the mayor or city attorney. To make matters worse, she copied one of the suspects, Capt. Hess, in her "no-go" letter to me.

Who gave Stokes the order not to farm it out to an outside law firm as she had recommended? What happened to that idea? The city wasn't about to let any outside investigative agency see any part of this case if they could help it. I sent an email to Stokes on December 13 saying I hoped she didn't share any of the evidence I provided her with to Hess, but I believe she might have. This was as bad as the attorney-client privilege game Capt. Hess and Lyon played when they "advised" Parker. Apparently, sharing evidence with suspects in power is how the City of Minneapolis rolls.

I forwarded my December 13, 2015, email from Stokes and my reply, along with additional blistering comments, to Mayor Hodges, the entire Minneapolis City Council, and the head of Human Resources. I received not one reply—not one word. I had just slammed a human resources "investigator" for seemingly compromising a sensitive human resources case, and nobody said a word. Not a word. All the cowards in power were now in hiding.

This is all the more evidence that a RICO case is the only answer to the City of Minneapolis's corruption problem. I was livid, and I sent another detailed email at 10:05 p.m. to the mayor and city council. I listed twelve scorching bullet points and concluded with "If the City Attorney or any of her assistants try and tell you anything to the contrary they are lying. I can and will show you the evidence."

I told the council members that, as city lawmakers, they were entitled to review this case and I had nothing to hide. I told them, "You can ask me anything you want. Also, if they try to tell you this is linked to my arbitration, they are delusional. This is about cops and federal agents who belong in prison." I received no reply from anyone. Dead silence.

Now, four years after being accused of being disruptive, I showed them what being disruptive was all about. No one ever said a word. I intentionally disrespected everyone on the city council and the mayor, and nobody said a thing. Not a word. The question is, Why? I told them their police department was riddled with corruption and gave them detailed bullet points regarding it. Who was telling everyone to keep quiet?

If all of this wasn't disgusting enough, Capt. Reed was still denying me the Medal of Valor for chasing down a man with a gun in December 2015 following a gang shootout after bar closing in downtown Minneapolis. In another case he denied me an award for tracking down a man who raped a ten-year-old girl. Officers under my command and I went above and beyond the call of duty and tracked the rapist down in St. Paul, and the city just spat on us.

CHAPTER 16
US SENATE JUDICIARY

On January 25, 2016, I kept up the pressure and sent Mayor Hodges a detailed two-page email outlining how I thought assistant City attorney David Nelson misled Judge Doty during the summary judgment. I also told Hodges about how I and my officers caught a rape suspect and my officers were denied a department award for going above and beyond the call of duty to catch the suspect, who had fled to St. Paul. I also told her about how I was put in for the Medal of Valor after chasing down a man with a gun seconds after a gang shootout in downtown Minneapolis. Hodges never replied, but I persisted and demanded the city at least recognize my officers.

The police department finally gave the officers a letter of appreciation rather than a department award of merit for tracking down a rapist. They clearly warranted higher recognition, but it was typical for the MPD to degrade good work and praise misconduct. The entire police department was out of sync. Hodges finally ordered Reed and his supervisors to give me the Medal of Valor in 2017, but think about it for a minute. Shots were fired, a person was shot, people were running for cover, it was a chaotic scene, and through it all I saw one of the suspects with a gun, and I chased the young man down a dark alley in a big city at two in the morning, and by the grace of God, at the very last spit second, I spared the kid's life and did not shoot him. Nevertheless, MPD commanders and city leaders denied me the

Medal of Valor for years. If this, in and of itself, does not reflect the dysfunction in the City of Minneapolis and the MPD, nothing does. Sadly, it explains at lot, and when a city and its police department abuse their police officers who put their lives on the line every day, invariably bad things will happen.

On March 2016, Sen. Grassley's attorney, Jay Lim, requested additional information, so on April 5, I sent Lim seven additional pages detailing corruption. Mr. Lim wasted no time, and by August 9 the FBI finally had the case. It was routed to the FBI's Criminal Investigation Division / Public Corruption Unit. The FBI told me they would be in touch.

U.S. Department of Justice

Federal Bureau of Investigation

Washington, D.C. 20535-0001

August 9, 2016

Mr. Michael P. Keefe

Dear Mr. Keefe:

      Your complaint directed to the Department of Justice, Office of the Inspector General (OIG), was referred to the Initial Processing Unit (IPU), Internal Investigations Section (IIS), Inspection Division (INSD), Federal Bureau of Investigation (FBI). The IIS/INSD is the FBI entity responsible for investigating allegations of misconduct or criminal activity on the part of FBI employees.

      In your complaint, you reported corruption involving members of the Violent Offender Task Force, along with Assistant U.S. Attorneys and Assistant Minneapolis City Attorneys. You claimed you filed a law suit against the Minneapolis Police Department (MPD) for corruption; however, the judge did not rule in your favor because the MPD and the Department of Justice refused to help you expose any wrongdoing.

      The purpose of this letter is to advise you the IIS/INSD has reviewed this matter and determined it does not warrant the opening of an administrative inquiry. This matter was forwarded to the Criminal Investigative Division, Public Corruption/Civil Rights Section for appropriate attention. IPU will take no further action in this matter.

Sincerely,

Unit Chief
Initial Processing Unit
Internal Investigations Section
Inspection Division

(August 9, 2016 FBI letter)

On August 17, eight days after the FBI notified me my case was with the Inspections Division, I asked Mayor Hodges to relieve the suspect officers from duty. I specifically asked Hodges to relieve from duty Parker, Reed, Wagner, Hess, Shaw, and all the other VOTF officers I believed were involved, but Hodges never did a thing. She never even replied.

On August 24, 2016, I asked Mayor Hodges and the city council to send letters of support to the FBI in seeking criminal charges for the involved officers in his case. It's unknown whether any of them did, but my guess is that they all did absolutely nothing. They didn't care about a cop who stood up for the rules of criminal procedure. Not only that, but I suspect they were scared of the FBI, and perhaps rightly so. The FBI sent more than one of them off to federal prison in recent years. James Comey was the director of the FBI when I asked the FBI for the second time to do their job and hold bad agents, attorneys, and cops accountable, but like his predecessor, Robert Mueller, his administration did nothing as well. Retired FBI agent Dan Vogel wasn't the least bit surprised. Vogel felt it was all about the FBI image, and exposing bad FBI agents wasn't a priority then, and according to Vogel, it never will be.

So the mayor of Minneapolis and the entire city council, which included today's mayor, Jacob Frey, had all been put on notice regarding the alleged corruption. They were given examples and details of the alleged corruption, but apparently not one of them ever did a thing. The police department was in peril, and they just looked the other way. I made it clear to them that a city attorney had allegedly provided false testimony to the federal court, and I gave them evidence of the alleged misconduct. Cops and attorneys were operating with absolute impunity, and nobody cared. It was a formula for disaster. They had big mouths when they could use the media to hype themselves up, but they wanted nothing to do with their dysfunctional police department. They simply did not care.

The FBI never got back to me. What in the world was going on? I had a spotless military record and a glowing police career that included being investigator of the year. I had documentation from two other officers and an FBI agent corroborating my complaint, but the FBI was silent. Not a word. Nothing. Was this really the United States, the country I served in the US Air Force; the country my dad served in the US Army; the country my uncle served as a Navy SEAL; the country my cousin died for on the beaches of Normandy as a US Army lieutenant, and a doctor no less; and the country for which another uncle of mine who was a marine was shot multiple times on Peleliu Island in the Pacific during World War II? Had the FBI become a rogue group of criminals with badges who were delusional enough to think they were untouchable? Or maybe they are. Many would argue we have a two-tiered system of justice in America today. Were they routinely covering the tracks of cops, agents, and attorneys who miscarried? It's a valid question that warrants serious review, because to date they have never done their job with my case. They have failed to police themselves, and that makes them a dangerous arm of our government. I had my case in front of FBI Inspections on two separate occasions, in 2009 and again in 2016, and both times they did nothing. Who were the decision makers that shut down those complaints? Robert Mueller was the Director of the FBI in 2009, James Comey was the Director of the FBI in 2016, and Christopher Wray became the Director of the FBI in 2017. Were these men deeply involved, or not involved at all? Its a question that needs to be answered because the final decision maker was either duped by unethical subordinates, or he willingly engaged in a coverup.

On April 6, 2017, I had my arbitration hearing for my unjust demotion. A demotion for reporting Parker and his boys to the Justice Department. A demotion for refusing to cover up exculpatory evidence. No matter what lie the city came up with, I was demoted for refusing to cover up evidence, and a corrupt Internal Affairs investigator and her supervisors framed me.

The assistant city attorney handling the arbitration was Ernest Lyon. Lyon advised the union that his witness would be former Maj. Yates. Why in the world would they bring back Yates? He had been gone from the MPD for several years. It made no sense, and I believed he had potential criminal culpability. Something wasn't right. Yates was sitting right next to Deputy Chief Parker in August 2007 when he admitted the cover story was a hoax. How could he be a credible witness? The police union and I were confused, so we requested the entire hearing be audio and video recorded. But the city objected, and the arbitrator agreed. That was the first red flag.

The arbitration started out, and I sat right across from Lyon. I felt right away there was nothing good about Lyon. Lyon just offered up Yates for slaughter because he apparently didn't care or he didn't have anyone else dumb enough to step up. Regardless, Yates proceeded to repeat the cover story, and he steadfastly swore it was the gospel. He went into great detail about how I made an unauthorized disclosure and compromised a wiretap and everything else it seemed to me he could dream up. Obviously nobody told him the FBI, according to Shaw and a retired BCA agent, had confirmed the story was completely unfounded—or he knew and he just didn't care because he and his cronies had nothing to lose. Yates arrogantly claimed I made an unauthorized disclosure despite the fact it never happened. Now I knew why the city did not want any audio or video recordings. The city's witness had come to the table, and the city was willing to protect him—as long as there wasn't a tape.

Once again, and now for a third time, the issue of a tape recording came into play. The first tape drama story was all about whether or not I taped anyone. The city and feds were obsessed with it. The second tape drama story was Shaw's claim that she had me on tape claiming officers and agents were being indicted, but apparently nobody cared about that alleged tape because it never existed. Now the third tape drama was about making sure nobody taped anything during my arbitration. Naturally, the city didn't want any of that on tape.

Keep in mind that this wasn't some reckless, unethical fly-by-night company I was fighting. It was the City of Minneapolis, the governing body of a major metropolitan city in America, and they decided how and when to play by the rules.

Yates was adamant I should never be a lieutenant. This was the same commander who told me and a union representative he would give me back my rank. The police union representative testified under oath that Yates said he would give me back my rank, but now Yates was saying I should never get my rank back. He repeated the stupid cover story that I believed everyone else knew was an absolute fabrication, but why? And who had recruited him to come back? The only good thing for me was that Yates had just extended the statute of limitations on a Title 18 conspiracy to obstruct justice case and much more.

Yates had offered me my rank back years earlier, shortly after I believe he and Parker had taken it to shut me up. The police union representative had given a deposition in the fall of 2011 and testified that Yates had told him he would give me back my rank. This is not to mention that Reed testified that Yates was allegedly the one who told him to write the phony performance improvement plan, which I believed was nothing more than a pretext to keep me from exposing MPD corruption to the Justice Department and other outside agencies. Yet he was their star witness? I thought Yates, Parker, and others were in deep, and he stepped up to be the big man on campus.

According to union attorney Ann Walther, I was precluded from bringing up Yates's promise to me and the union representative, so we did what she said and kept it off the table. Walther told me and the police union that the city objected to any and all video and audio recording. There was nothing we could do except bring in additional witnesses, so that's what we did. We brought in three police union representatives. All three listened to Yates repeat the cover story and claim I made an unauthorized disclosure. Yates carried on as though he didn't have a care in the world.

Walther gave my case to Erick Ball, a young attorney in her office. He was a nice man and a top notch attorney. Ball did the best he could with his hands basically tied behind his back, but I lost the arbitration after the arbitrator fell for Yates's story that I made an unauthorized disclosure and compromised a federal case. Yates essentially insisted the cover story was legitimate. Ball and I told the arbitrator that was not true, but he apparently didn't believe it. We left the arbitration hearing in shock. The MPD was filthy from the top down.

It turns out the arbitrator was a law professor, not a licensed attorney in Minnesota according to the Minnesota lawyers professional responsibility board. He seemed mesmerized by Yates just because he was a licensed schoolteacher. He did rule in my favor that VOTF officers lied, but I thought he just could not figure the case out. He seemed confused. Common sense would dictate that if the cops lied about one thing, they lied about another, but this arbitrator seemed totally lost. He seemed clueless—so clueless, in fact, that he ruled that I did not follow the orders of the ATF. Police do not take orders from federal agents or their supervisors except when they are on a task force, and on this task force, I was the commander of everyone. It was in black-and-white in the bylaws, which he was given a copy of to review.

The arbitrator's ruling should have resulted in the immediate suspension and termination of the cops who lied to Internal Affairs, but the MPD didn't care about that, because they were all seemingly protected by Parker and Reed. Naturally there was no follow-up MPD investigation.

After I lost my arbitration, that was it. I was done. The arbitrator's ruling came down on May 17, 2017, and I was done right there and then. No more fighting these criminals with badges and cowards in power. I gave them their city. I was done putting my life on the line for people masquerading as legitimate leaders and police officers. I retired and literally burned my uniforms. I wanted nothing to remind me of all the years of hell I had gone through fighting these rotten bastards. The dirty cops, FBI agents, and attorneys won.

Years earlier, when I was standing in the back of the First Precinct in downtown Minneapolis, Minneapolis assistant city attorney Tom Miller told me, "You broke the code." Miller was right. I did break the code, and I'd do it again without hesitation. It was the first time I had ever met Mr. Miller, so I assumed it was the running joke in the city attorney's office. Assistant city attorney Ray Cantu was standing next to Miller when he made that remark.

In retrospect, it's hard to believe that an attorney in the United States can stand in front of a US District Court judge and an appeals court and, in my opinion, steadfastly spew seemingly false statements with malicious intent and get away with it, but that's exactly what I believe Nelson did. The transcript of the taped hearing at the Eighth Circuit Court confirmed that Nelson said what he said. I believe Nelson committed fraud upon the court when he seemingly misled Judge Doty and the Eighth Circuit Court of Appeals.

If the FBI was not involved in the media attacks and helping assistant US attorneys and Shaw with the outlandish and reprehensible Internal Affairs debacle in 2008, they should be doing everything they can to take down the cops and attorneys who did. Denton implied they were in on the media attacks, so an honest investigation would at least give the FBI an opportunity to clear their name and step away from those cowardly deeds and set the record straight if they're innocent. The only problem is that an investigation would expose those two high-ranking FBI agents who stabbed me in the back and their supervisors, as well as any assistant US attorneys who assisted them, and the FBI wants those secrets buried forever.

There are several others in the city of Minneapolis who deserve severe punishment and perhaps termination, but unfortunately they can't send the cowardly politicians who blamed everything on street cops to prison for being snakes.

But make no mistake about it. The failure of elected Minneapolis city officials to do their jobs was a major contributing factor in the tsunami that hit Minneapolis after the death of George Floyd. What I believed was the deliberate indifference of the city council and at least two mayors likely allowed the so-called leaders of the MPD to turn the department into a good ole boys and girls club. Meanwhile, all the good cops were cast aside and treated like dirt.

On July 15, 2017, Minneapolis police officer Mohamed Noor and his partner responded to a possible assault call in one of the safest neighborhoods in Minneapolis. Noor was the passenger officer, and as he and his partner drove down an alley looking for a suspect, the 911 caller ran up to the squad car and allegedly slapped the back of the car to get them to stop and talk to her. Noor drew his gun, reached across in front of his partner, and fired his weapon. He killed the unarmed 911 caller, Justine Damond.

The event made national news, and everyone was in shock—except me and other cops who had been trying to expose the flaws and corruption inside the MPD for years. The message to bad cops in Minneapolis who had friends in high places was clear: "We've got your back. You can do whatever you want. We will take care of you." Mohamed Noor was the MPD's latest golden child, as the police administration did everything they could to win over the Somali community in Minneapolis. Unfortunately, phony politics may have sent Noor the wrong message. When Noor shot and killed Justine Damon, the Minneapolis police administration never gave the high-profile case any special attention. They were all too busy reviewing their social media accounts. Medaria Arradondo had risen to deputy chief and was quickly promoted to chief after the senseless and horrible shooting of Justine Damond, but the corruption problem had not been solved, and like an untreated cancer, it continued to fester.

After I retired, I tried to move on with my life. But I knew I could still help the city and the good cops put the bad cops, agents, and attorneys in prison if I could get someone to do his or her job. So on December 19, 2018, I asked Minnesota senator Amy Klobuchar for help. I sent Klobuchar's attorney, Elizabeth Farrer, a thirteen-page letter summarizing the corruption. Sen. Klobuchar's legal team demanded answers from the FBI, and they responded, but their response on February 14, 2019, was more of the same—straight hogwash. In no uncertain terms, the FBI lied and said everything had been reviewed. The old "reviewed" game, just like the City of Minneapolis, and nobody signed the letter. Funny how that works when government agencies are lying. A wink and a nod and a "We're all good here, right? Nobody sign anything. Perfect! Okay, let's go have lunch and take the rest of the afternoon off."

U.S. Department of Justice

Federal Bureau of Investigation

Washington, D. C. 20535-0001

February 14, 2019

Mr. Mike Keefe

Dear Mr. Keefe:

    Your complaint addressed to Elizabeth Farrer of Senator Amy Klobuchar's office in Washington, District of Columbia, was referred to the Initial Processing Unit (IPU), Internal Affairs Section (IAS), Inspection Division (INSD), Federal Bureau of Investigation (FBI). The IAS/INSD is the FBI entity responsible for investigating allegations of misconduct or criminal activity on the part of FBI employees.

    In your complaint, you reported the Federal Bureau of Investigation, along with other law enforcement entities, failed to investigate information you provided regarding public corruption and overtime fraud abuse, pertaining to employees within the Minneapolis Police Department. You reported those entities were responsible for your employment termination as a Minneapolis, Minnesota police officer, wherein you cited racial discrimination and a possible cover-up of the information you provided.

    The purpose of this letter is to advise you the IAS/INSD has thoroughly reviewed this matter and determined this matter does not warrant the opening of an FBI inquiry. IPU will take no further action in this matter.

Sincerely,

Initial Processing Unit
Internal Affairs Section
Inspection Division

(Senator Klobuchar) 2/14/2019

Christopher Wray was the acting FBI director on February 14, 2019, which was the same day the acting US attorney general, Matthew Whitaker, stepped down and was replaced by William Barr. Was this just a coincidence, or did the FBI intentionally slip their seemingly patently false response to Senator Klobuchar past the outgoing acting attorney general before he left and Barr took control of the justice department? It's a reasonable question considering the totality of the circumstances. Senator Klobuchar is a powerful US senator, and the sooner the FBI got her off their back, the better.

Minnesota Rep. Jason Lewis, like Senator Klobuchar, did a nice job in seeking answers from the FBI as well, but like Klobuchar, he was stonewalled. Was the FBI intentionally being deceitful, or were they just asleep at the wheel and too lazy to do their job?

On February 14, 2019, after I sought the help of Senator Klobuchar, the FBI sent me a letter saying my complaint was "thoroughly reviewed"; but if they had at least looked at it even briefly, they would have known I wasn't fired. The letter claimed I had been fired. I retired. It was obvious to me the case was shelved. The FBI wanted nothing to do with a case involving their own agents and attorneys. I wasn't surprised by the FBI's reckless and arrogant claim, so on April 14, 2019, I appealed the FBI's so-called "thoroughly reviewed" claim to the new US Senate judiciary chairman, Lyndsey Graham. I sent Senator Graham two letters, the first letter on April 14, 2019 (five pages), and the second on May 29, 2019 (two pages); but unlike Chairman Grassley, who immediately took command and control, Sen. Graham never responded. What did Mr. Graham do with my letters? Christopher Wray was the FBI Director in 2019.

CHAPTER 17
MAYOR FREY

ON MAY 3, 2019, THE CITY OF MINNEAPOLIS SETTLED THE JUSTINE Damond civil suit and paid her family $20 million. On May 21, I sent Minneapolis Mayor Frey, Chief Arradondo, and the Minneapolis city council the first of six letters detailing corruption in the MPD. Five of the six letters were sent in May and June of 2019, almost exactly a year to the day before the in-custody death of George Floyd. I sent another letter in June of 2020 after the in-custody death of George Floyd. All six letters were sent to Mayor Frey, and the city council and chief were copied on three of them.

The six letters were sent on May 21, 2019; June 4, 2019; June 6, 2019; June 14, 2019; June 18, 2019; and June 9, 2020.

The 2019 letters spelled everything out loud and clear to Mayor Frey, Chief Arradondo, and the city council. None of them ever replied. Why wasn't something done? Who was responsible for repeatedly shutting down every single attempt at accountability and transparency?

Before I sent my letters to the mayor, I sent detailed letters about the corruption to the new MPD Internal Affairs commander, Lieutenant Tom Wheeler. Wheeler was an honorable man, and I had absolutely no doubt he forwarded the letters up the chain of command. After I sent my first letter to Mayor Frey on May 21, 2019, I received a letter back from the Minneapolis Office of Police Conduct Review dated May 22, 2019. The letter claimed the MPD had **"no jurisdiction" because the complaint did not involve Minneapolis officers.** What? Why were they lying? Clearly nothing had changed in the MPD, and nobody was dumb enough to personally sign that letter, but it was closed with "Sincerely, Joint Supervisors Office of Police Conduct Review."

My May 21, 2019, letter was six pages long and identified Sgt. Shaw and other current and former Minneapolis police officers and assistant city attorneys as suspects who allegedly engaged in egregious misconduct. Nevertheless, the Office of Police Conduct Review claimed they did not have any jurisdiction. It made absolutely no sense. Several officers were still on the department, and to make it all the more bizarre, the letter admitted it had been reviewed by supervisors who were civilian and sworn. I had identified Shaw and others in this massive case of alleged corruption, and yet the Office of Police Conduct Review claimed they had no jurisdiction over Sgt. Shaw and others. My 2013 letters to Lt. Burke and Deputy Chief Lambert were irrefutable evidence of Shaw's direct involvement in everything, not to mention the entire file.

Minneapolis
City of Lakes

Office of Police Conduct Review

Civilian Unit
350 S. Fifth St. – Room 239
Minneapolis, MN 55415
TEL 612.673.5500

Internal Affairs Unit
350 S. Fifth St. – Room 112
Minneapolis, MN 55415
TEL 612.673.3074
www.minneapolismn.gov

May 22, 2019

Michael Keefe

Re: OPCR Case Number 19-07127

Dear Michael Keefe:

This letter is in regards to the complaint you filed on May 20, 2019 alleging police misconduct. Your complaint was jointly reviewed by Supervisors from the Civilian and Sworn units of the OPCR. After taking into consideration the evidence you provided along with that provided by the City of Minneapolis, the Office has decided not to proceed with your complaint for the following reasons:

No Jurisdiction
Unfortunately, the Office of Police Conduct Review will not be able to review the matter as the incident you described did not involve officers from the Minneapolis Police Department. However, if you wish to still pursue an investigation into the matter, we believe that you can contact the following organizations for assistance:

Minnesota Bureau of Criminal Apprehension OR Federal Bureau of Investigations
1430 Maryland Ave E
St. Paul, MN 55106
(651) 793-7000

1501 Freeway Boulevard
Brooklyn Center, MN 55430
(763) 569-8000

Sincerely,

Joint Supervisors
Office of Police Conduct Review

www.minneapolismn.gov
Affirmative Action Employer

(Letter from City Of Minneapolis, Police review, 5/22/19)

Mayor Frey never personally responded, but his office assistant, Zach Farley, responded on June 18, 2019, with "Our office will be unable to help with this matter." I responded, "I'm sorry Zach, but the Mayor has the power and authority to demand accountability. I don't understand?" That was the last communication between me and Mayor Frey's office.

So what did Mayor Frey do with the letters? Did he pass them on to the FBI? The letters outlined serious allegations of potential criminal misconduct. I believe Mayor Frey needs to be held accountable for those letters, which clearly outlined a number of potential crimes on the part of Minneapolis police officers, federal agents, and attorneys. The fourth letter in particular explained how I and many attorneys felt the crimes allegedly committed by the culpable officers, agents, and attorneys made it a potential RICO case.

Impartial attorneys believe the only way to get to the bottom of all the alleged corruption is a full scale criminal investigation with a special prosecutor and a team of experienced investigators that have no current or past connection to any of the involved parties. I believe one of the first things they should do is execute a search warrant on MPD Internal Affairs and demand Mayor Frey turn over those six letters I sent him. If he refuses, execute another search warrant, and last but not least, a congressional investigation of the FBI.

If there is no investigation or accountability, it will happen again in Minneapolis or some other city. A democracy that allows law enforcement officers to operate with impunity is no longer a democracy. It's a dictatorship.

On May 25, 2020, just a year and four days after I first asked Mayor Frey, Chief Arradondo, and the city council to step up and do something about corruption in the MPD, all hell broke loose. Third Precinct cops were videotaped by a civilian holding down a black man after a physical confrontation and he was telling them he was struggling to breathe. The man, George Floyd, died and the video went viral, and just like that the MPD was national news and the civil unrest tsunami hit Minneapolis.

The very next day, May 26, 2020, Dr. Andrew Baker, Hennepin County's chief medical examiner, conducted a preliminary autopsy of

Mr. Floyd and noted he had heart disease, Covid, and the drug fentanyl in his system. Further examination revealed his lungs were at least twice their normal weight at autopsy.

In court Dr. Baker testified that if Floyd had been home alone in his locked residence with no evidence of trauma and the only autopsy finding was his fentanyl level, he would certify his death as due to fentanyl toxicity. However, Dr. Baker also testified that in his opinion the law enforcement subdual restraint and neck compression was more than Floyd could take by virtue of his heart condition. Dr. Baker classified Floyd's cause of death as a homicide, but he noted, "Homicide in my world is a medical term; it's not a legal term."

Doctors and lawyers will always argue about Floyd's cause of death, murder or manslaughter? But nobody can argue the Minneapolis Police Department was a paramilitary organization with an established rank structure, and like the military, you follow orders and do what you are told. On May 25, 2020 three rookie MPD officers, Thomas Lane, Alexander Kueng, and Tou Thao, did what they were told and followed the orders of their superior officer, Derek Chauvin, but they were given all the wrong orders. Lane questioned the orders, but he was rebuffed twice when he appropriately suggested turning Floyd on his side. Chauvin refused to take Lane's advice and within a matter of minutes Floyd died.

So everything comes back full circle to the dysfunctional MPD. Four officers at a critical incident, three of them rookies, and no supervisor. It was a formula for disaster. Years of corruption exploded like a nuclear bomb and three rookie cops who had nothing to do with the corruption went down with the ship. According to defense attorneys, the rookie cops should have been shielded from criminal prosecution after Lane clearly objected to Chauvin's orders, but that never happened. The MPD was a national disgrace and the rookie cops were an easy target.

Mayor Frey and his predecessor, Becky Hodges, were not making any quick and decisive legal decisions, they had plenty of time to ponder the multiple problems I warned them about inside the police department. Mayor Hodges said she merely passed everything off to the city attorney, and admitted that's all she did. Wow! Talk about leadership. And what about Mayor Frey? What did he do with the letters I gave him? Did he follow the party line and dump them off on the city attorney?

If the MPD and FBI had acted on my complaints, Sgt. Burt's complaints, FBI agent O'Shea's complaint, and assistant US attorney Hanson's complaint, the whole culture of the MPD might have changed.

Maybe, just maybe, if the politicians, police commanders, and FBI had done something when I and Sgt. Burt first complained about corruption, Officer Noor might have kept his pistol in his holster in 2017 and maybe Officer Chauvin might have listened to Officer Lane.

All the wrong signals and messages were sent to Officers Noor and Chauvin, and every other officer in the department. When a police department persecutes its whistleblowers and rewards bad cops, sooner or later officers take risks and make bad decisions. Noor and Chauvin took risks and made bad decisions, and it cost them their freedom. Minneapolis police officers had poor leadership for years, and they were sent all the wrong signals. It was a police department driving with the lights off, bound to crash—and crash it did, big time.

If the MPD had listened to me and Sgt. Burt and prosecuted every officer involved in our Internal Affairs complaints, it would have sent a completely different message to the rank and file. It would have set the bar high, and officers would have known in no uncertain terms what the ground rules were and where they stood. Cops would never have rolled the dice. But that never happened.

The lack of accountability and transparency turned the MPD into a ticking time bomb, and that bomb, despite repeated warnings, exploded on May 25, 2020. After the city imploded, its leaders blamed the police union for protecting bad cops. But the police union did everything possible to protect the good cops from the bad cops. I believe it was the elected officials who protected the bad cops; they did so by not supporting me and Burt. The rank-and-file officers knew what I and Sgt. Burt were fighting for, and when the chief, mayor, and city council refused to back us up, it sent all the wrong messages. Doomsday was inevitable.

The problem wasn't the police union. The problem in my mind

was the mayors, police commanders, assistant city attorneys, the city council, and, last but not least, the FBI. If any of them had sat down and listened to Burt and me, they would have discovered that some of the police officers in this case had long histories of misconduct. They would have also discovered that an FBI agent I believe played a major role in this case was written up for serious misconduct, and that would have just been the tip of the iceberg.

Speaking of past mayors, Betsy Hodges got her nose back into the political spotlight after the George Floyd fiasco. She took time out of her busy schedule to tell the *New York Times* on July 10, 2020, that "as Mayor of Minneapolis, I saw how white liberals block change." She also accused the police of "standing guard" over white neighborhoods while aggressively patrolling black neighborhoods to provide a wall of protection around white people and their property. This was the same mayor who declined to read three detailed letters of corruption while she was mayor. Maybe if she had read those letters and done something, that so-called "wall of protection" might have come down.

Carter Reed also threw his hat into the national media "look-at-me" three-ring circus after the Floyd fiasco. Reed told a newspaper the George Floyd in-custody death was a result of "systemic racism" in police forces across the country. So what did he do to stop it? Seemingly nothing.

In March 2021, the City of Minneapolis paid out $27 million to the family of George Floyd. In 2019 the city paid Justine Damond's family $20 million. The city went to great lengths to cover up the misconduct that I and others exposed. The city desperately tried to bury me and avoid a settlement with my attorneys. Sadly, a settlement with me and my attorneys coupled with accountability may very well have prevented everything. It would have been peanuts compared to all the subsequent death and destruction that followed the Floyd fiasco.

The City of Minneapolis could have settled my case if they had listened to me and Sgt. Burt and made significant changes. Instead they presumably chose to lie and cover it all up. That backfired to the tune of $47 million taxpayer dollars.

CONCLUSION

When Sgt. Burt and I "broke the code," as so eloquently stated by Minneapolis assistant city attorney Tom Miller, we stepped out onto an island, and I was repeatedly assaulted by my peers who were in positions of power. I can't speak for Sgt. Burt, but no law enforcement officer anywhere in the country should ever have to endure the abuse I went through simply for refusing to cover up evidence. I didn't care whether the focus was cops or a career drug dealer; I wasn't about to cover up any evidence, and neither was Sgt. Burt.

I suspect the involved cops, agents, and attorneys repeatedly tipped each other off every step of the way as they accused me of the crimes they likely committed. The chance encounter between me and Sgt. Burt in the Minneapolis police property and evidence room was a godsend for me and very likely stopped them. I wholeheartedly believe FBI agents helped the Minneapolis PD frame me. I also believe assistant US attorneys and assistant Minneapolis city attorneys helped them get the job done, and MPD Internal Affairs and FBI Inspections covered it all up. To frame someone is to make a person seem to be guilty of a crime by providing false information. There was no shortage of false information and I believe it was a team effort. They destroyed my career, my reputation, and nearly my family. They demoted me and laughed all the way to the bank. The evidence is overwhelming and irrefutable. Law enforcement officers and attorneys who have reviewed the facts of this case feel strongly, as do I, that the culpable parties behind this massive case of intentional and calculated criminal misconduct should face multiple criminal charges.

The mere thought of law enforcement officers and attorneys covering up evidence to frame innocent police officers and anyone who stood up for them is scary business. If they were willing to frame fellow officers, they would frame anyone, and maybe they did. The last criminal act appears to have occurred in 2017 or, more likely, as recently as July 2020, when FBI agents and a southern Minnesota county sheriff attempted to intimidate me after the George Floyd fiasco, so the FBI still has plenty of time to do its job and prove it's an honorable law enforcement agency. Not to mention the potential tolling of criminal statutes. Tolling statutes is a legal precedent that stops the clock on the statute of limitations.

When Minneapolis imploded, the mayor and city council froze and the Third Precinct burned. The events of that day set off violent protests around the country, and Minneapolis was the epicenter of it all.

After the dust settled, Minneapolis politicians continued to claim everything was a direct result of the police union protecting bad cops for years, but that was nothing but political garbage. I believe the politicians were desperately trying to cover their tracks. Years of dirty deeds on the part of city leaders and police commanders was the cause and effect, not the police union. The police union steadfastly supported me and Burt. The problem wasn't the police union. The problem was some elected officials and high-ranking police commanders. The city of Minneapolis was literally burning to the ground, and the powers that be adopted the mantra, "Admit nothing, deny everything, and counteraccuse."

They never once mentioned that righteous police officers and federal agents had warned them repeatedly for years about internal problems and rogue cops. It was time to cover their political careers, but the good cops weren't fooled one bit. Retirements set an all-time record, and good cops left the city.

The law-abiding citizens of Minneapolis were left with a severely wounded police department that lost at least 170 officers in one year, and crime skyrocketed. Officers bailed from the city that was repeatedly blaming them for the mess they created, and who could blame them? The city forgot about all the cops who chased people down dark alleys, through yards, and over fences with guns and never opened fire. There were plenty of them, but it didn't matter. In the eyes of the city and national so-called leaders they were all bad.

The City of Minneapolis protected bad cops for years, and they were blaming the police union and systemic racism for all the problems. But let's not forget that it was the white mayors, the white city council members, the white assistant city attorneys, the white police commanders, the white FBI agents, and the white assistant US attorneys who, I believe, helped covered the tracks of the bad white cops, agents, and attorneys. The white rank-and-file officers and the predominately white police union had nothing to do with all the misconduct, cover-ups, witness tampering, threats, intimidation, extortion, and phony propaganda emails. It was the powers that be who were culpable for all those crimes—yes, crimes—not the street cops or the police union.

They not only destroyed my career and reputation, but they discredited two very intelligent, dedicated, and honest African American attorneys' careers and reputations for alleging they brought about a frivolous and bogus civil suit in representing me.

Within a year the police force was so depleted the chief had to ask for the assistance of local, state, and federal agencies to combat the rising crime. Minneapolis was in chaos and getting worse every day.

On May 4, 2021, I sent a rough draft of this book to Acting US Attorney General Merrick Garland. The Justice Department acknowledged the manuscript three months later, on August 13, 2021, but did nothing to follow up. It's a secret they want buried forever.

When it comes to dirty secrets, the City of Minneapolis has plenty of its own. Remember the Minneapolis police deputy chief's email from the spring of 2009? "We will vigorously investigate any and all allegations of corruption. There is no acceptable degree of corruption in law enforcement." And who could forget Mayor Hodges's propaganda letter on February 10, 2014, which stated, "We hold our city leaders to the highest standard. This is the policy of the city, and the policy will be enforced."

In the end, it was a relentless salvo of misinformation and deception on the part of high-ranking cops, FBI supervisors, attorneys, and, I believe, elected officials. When the cameras were rolling, there was a consistent theme: "The cops on the street are the problem, and so is the police union." It was all baloney. The powers that be were literally out of control, and the citizens of Minneapolis were the victims. In due time, the whole country would become a victim. What started out as a rotten, hate-filled attack quickly turned into a cowardly tsunami of lies and deceit. At times it was haphazard, and, at other times, it was meticulous and cunning. Regardless of the strategy, the ranking FBI or DOJ official who gave the Minneapolis FBI field office the green light to carry out the attack needs to be identified and prosecuted along with all the officers, agents, and attorneys who willingly followed that illegal order. Three rookie officers are in prison for unwillingly following orders so whats the difference? The difference I believe is those three rookie officers didn't have the power and authority of the Justice Department backing them up.

In August 2021, retired FBI agent Dan Vogel sent me a card after he read the rough draft of this book while it was in the process of being vetted for production. In the card Vogel wrote, "Mike, thanks for all you have done to seek the truth. May God bless! Dan V."

Corruption is like a slow-moving cancer; initially it's difficult to identify, but eventually everything becomes very clear. But by the time it becomes clear, it is too late, and it destroys everything in its path. Corruption destroyed the city of Minneapolis in 2020, and the people responsible for it are either still employed or are enjoying healthy government pensions.

In March of 2022, the Wilder Research company released a review of the city's response to the unrest following the in-custody death of George Floyd, and this review wasted no time pointing out that the city lacked leadership and failed to coordinate with responding state agencies who arrived to help. The report said there were conflicting orders and a lack of "clear, experienced" leadership.

The city of Minneapolis lacked a lot of things—most importantly, accountability. In the end, it was nothing but chaos and mayhem. Large parts of the city burned, people died, and it all could have been avoided.